Revealing Antiquity

· 4 ·

G. W. Bowersock, General Editor

A Chronicle
of the Last Pagans

PIERRE CHUVIN

Translated by
B. A. Archer

HARVARD UNIVERSITY PRESS
CAMBRIDGE, MASSACHUSETTS
LONDON, ENGLAND
1990

This book is a translation of part 1 of
Chronique des derniers païens,
published by Librairie Arthème Fayard
and
Société d'Edition Les Belles Lettres in 1990.

Library of Congress Cataloging-in-Publication Data

Chuvin, Pierre.
A chronicle of the last pagans / Pierre Chuvin : translated
by B. A. Archer.
p. cm.—(Revealing antiquity : 4)

1. Paganism—Rome. 2. Christianity—Early church, ca.
30–600. 3. Christianity and other religions—History—
Roman. 4. Rome—Civilization. 5. Civilization, Oriental.
I. Title. II. Series.
BR128.R7C58 1990
292'.009'015—dc20   89-20091
                                                    CIP

"A pool of silence and a tower of grace"
—W. H. Auden

· *ACKNOWLEDGMENTS* ·

My search for the last pagans of classical Antiquity originally was a voyage all of whose difficulties were not—are they ever?—of a scientific nature. Some auspicious stars shone in a sometimes cloudy sky:

—had not G. W. Bowersock expected the book, it would have remained in my files;

—had not Michel and Marie-Pierre Tardieu, in Paris, been, with all the former's learning, so warm and friendly, it would have been written with less pleasure;

—had not, for years, Stéphane Khémis and Valérie Hannin, at *L'Histoire*, given me opportunities to popularize ancient history, perhaps it could have been read only by fellow scholars, who probably have little to learn from it.

Finally I wish to thank Michel Desgranges, director of the French publishing house Les Belles Lettres; Ann Louise C. McLaughlin, who made my work on the English translation a pleasure; and Professors Francis Vian and Paul Bernard, who patiently agreed that projects dear to us—Nonnus' edition and the study of the friezes on the rhytons from Nisa—might be delayed to allow me that simple praise of obstinacy.

P.C.

· CONTENTS ·

A Chronicle of the Last Pagans

Introduction

IN CONSTANTINOPLE, now known as Istanbul and completely Islamicized, a visitor who toils up the hill to the former Church of the Pantocrator (where the rulers of the Comnenian and Palaeologan dynasties are buried) and the Mosque of the Conqueror (burial place of the first Turkish sultan of the city) passes on his right a humble tomb surrounded by a low fence, whitewashed and bordered in green paint—clearly of no aesthetic or historic interest. Beside the tomb, on the retaining wall of the hill, a sign has been posted by order of the city's directorate of muftis: "It is forbidden by Islam to light candles, tie ribbons, stick stones for vows, toss coins, or sacrifice victims. This is a sin."

This prohibition, found elsewhere in the city in front of tombs or on trees, is not altogether effective: bits of cloth are often tied to the fence. And yet, unintentionally and probably unknowingly, the promulgators of this injunction were reviving a law decreed in the same capital by the emperor Theodosius I on November 8, 392, nearly sixteen centuries ago: "No one, under any circumstances, is permitted to sacrifice an innocent victim nor, as a less serious sacrilege, to worship one's lares with fire, one's genius with uncut wine, one's penates with perfume, to light lamps, waft incense, or hang garlands."

Pagan rituals that are clearly identifiable as such have survived all the upheavals, all the campaigns for religious conversion, and all the homilies intended to purify the faith of the masses. The arrival in Anatolia of Turkish tribes from the Khorassan, beginning late in the eleventh century, by no means eradicated pagan customs. It only reinforced them, for these tribes, recently Islamicized, maintained similar customs. The enormous demographic changes that took place in Istanbul during this century, bringing to it a great influx of peasants, gave renewed vigor to these rituals in a city as holy for Muslims as for Orthodox Christians. The veneration inspired by that seemingly most ordinary grave is still accompanied by gestures far more ancient than the advent of Islam or the faded memory of Byzantium.

This short walk among tombs may be concluded by the simple observation that in the life of a people, as in the life of an individual, it is much easier to point out the first time an event occurred than the last. Although it is easy enough to follow the stages of Christianity's victory—and there is no doubt that its pagan adversaries were put to rout—it will always be risky to speak of "the last pagans." And yet it is worthwhile to take the viewpoint of the vanquished—those who seem to have been behind their own times—while bearing in mind that they did not consider themselves defeated or backward—unless they were ripe for conversion. In this examination of the customs and beliefs of pagans during the Christian period of the Roman Empire, let us forget that, for us, they were the last.

Let us also dispense with the notion that they lived in a period of decadence. Today we are too prone to believe that their world was dramatically collapsing. Accordingly, we readily attribute to the Romans of the fourth and fifth centuries A.D. our own deceptive lucidity, mixed with melancholy and the bitter resignation of "waiting for the Barbarians." The old prejudice about "decadence" has given rise to all kinds of misconceptions about an era as uncertain in its overtones as that lovely fragment of a fifth-century poem which scholars continue to discuss without being able to decide whether it describes the life-giving showers of spring or the squalls of autumn. In reality, never was imperial power more efficient, more absolute, more centralized. And the events that appear singularly ominous to our eyes—the invasions of the Huns or the Goths—would have appeared to contemporaries as difficulties of a familiar kind, which would have to be dealt with sooner or later in any case.

Around 430 a strange character, both poet and diplomat (or double agent), named Olympiodorus issued, in Greek, a contemporary history of the western Roman Empire. He included the terrible catastrophe of August 410, when the Visigoths, led by their king, Alaric, sacked Rome. However, the author chose to end his account in 425, when Theodosius II, reigning in Constantinople, restored the unity of the Empire by placing on the throne of Rome his son-in-law, Valentinian III, who ruled for thirty years—a generation. Of the two dates, 410 and 425, the first is obviously the more fateful today. But was this so when Olympiodorus was writing, when Rome was living under a ruler whose legitimacy was unimpeachable (he was descended both from Valentinian I and Theodosius I, two outstanding emperors of the second half of the fourth century)? How could the continuity of the Empire not appear to hold greater significance than Alaric's short-lived atrocities?

• • •

THE chronological boundaries of this book do not coincide with those that historians assign to the Christian Empire. That would take us much too far—all the way to 1204 (the capture of Constantinople by the Fourth Crusade, resulting in a major transformation of the Empire), or to 1453 (its ulti-mate demise when it fell to the Ottoman Turks). Nor do they fit the period labeled Late Antiquity, which begins with the reign of Diocletian (284–305), notable for a political reorgani-zation that was followed by the last persecutions (303–313) just before Christianity became the religion in power. The end of this period is usually dated too early in my view, at one time or other during the fifth century: between 410 (Alaric's sack of Rome) and 476 (Odoacer's insurrection), or the end of the century (the establishment of the Franks in Gaul, and the consolidation in the east of an empire, under Anastasius I, that was nothing more than "eastern").

The religious rulings of the emperors provide more appro-priate chronologies. The edicts of tolerance promulgated in 311–313 by Constantine and his colleagues on behalf of Chris-tians instituted a force that would never again be questioned, not even during the eighteen months of Julian's ultimately in-consequential reign fifty years later. Justinian's ban in 529, not only of pagan cults but also of pagan beliefs, could mark the final boundary of our inquiry, but minds are not that mallea-ble nor, fortunately, are laws that effective. The "inquisitions" instigated by Tiberius II (578–582) attest to a pagan resistance that may have lasted locally until the Arab conquest of the 630s and, in one region at least, continued under Muslim domination until the eleventh century. For the Byzantine world, the crisis that began after the death of Justinian (565) marks a sharp break with its Hellenic and pagan past. The collection of "brief historical notes" (that is its actual title) con-cerning Constantinople's statues written early in the eighth century illustrates, by its outlandish explanations, how much had been forgotten of the classical tradition by that time and how uncertain scholars had become.[1]

Dates are necessary, but one must guard against attaching too much importance to them. Among the many awesome events that punctuate the period from 312 to 429, none was able to break down the unity of Late Antique culture. At worst, that culture was progressively relegated to the Eastern Empire where, from the start, it had flourished most brilliantly. As Louis Robert remarked on reading the epigrams that honored the governors, "from the second part of the 3rd century to the end of the 6th, one finds the same themes, the same formulae, the same style."[2] In 359–360 a governor (proconsul) of Achaia, Ampelius, living in Corinth, decided to summer on the neighboring island of Aegina, where he built a private sanctuary to the Muses, shaded by plane trees and cooled by streams. Under a statue of the god Pan, he had engraved a tribute to the estate and to his own sense of justice. (For Ampelius this was a professional virtue: in Greek and in Latin governors were called "judges.") Pan addresses the passerby: "No longer do I delight in gamboling across the hills with my wax-bound pipes, nor in caves, nor under the dense foliage of trees; I no longer love Echo, nor do I take pleasure in the goatherds. Yearning for the magnificent works of a man of justice, Ampelius, I come leaping, delighted in a place where the Muses, enchanted by the plane trees and bubbling brooks, have made their abode."

This bucolic eulogy was composed during the reign of Constantius, when the temples were closed and traditional cults nearly prohibited. Was Ampelius escaping into a nostalgic dream world? Not at all. The various themes of the epigram remained current throughout Late Antiquity, whether it be the association of the Muses and Justice (which reappears a few years later in connection with another proconsul of Achaia, one of the most famous pagans of his time, Vettius Agorius Praetextatus, and also at the end of the fifth century in the encomium of a Christian high official, a pretorian prefect) or the evocation of the charms of a lovely place that attracts local divinities—most often baths frequented by Nymphs and Naiads, up to the sixth century.

Ampelius' traditionalism is genuine: "museums" of this

kind appeared in inscriptions at least since the Principate. And in his time, it is not peculiar to him. It attests to the care with which this society, across three centuries, preserved its heritage.[3] But whereas official inscriptions of the High Empire were generally in prose, from then on they no less generally became epigrams.[4] Poetry, with its pageant of images and pagan themes, took over as never before, as will be verified when we follow the careers of poets. In addition to poetry, law, philosophy, and rhetoric also ranked high. During these centuries learning maintained its prestige and schools continued to prosper, even in the West, so long as a modicum of Roman order survived there.

For pagans, what was different was the necessity of adapting to a completely unparalleled situation. No longer were their religion and their rituals those of the state. This was a situation to inspire nostalgia and attempts at winning back their lost public privileges, and also to hasten the spread, beginning in the third century, of beliefs and practices of a private nature, under the influence of philosophy (Platonic and Pythagorean), former initiation cults (official ones like the Eleusinian mysteries or less formal ones like Orphism), and "Chaldean" or "Egyptian" magic.

The complementarity of such factors, so strange to modern eyes, makes the pagan religiosity of these two centuries a phenomenon well worth studying for its own sake. Starting from there we can see how some kind of paganism branched out and survived until modern times, either as humble superstitious rites or as the very subtle Neoplatonic mysticism of a Marsilio Ficino. As for the paganism of our contemporaries who style themselves "new pagans," this more often than not perverse form of romanticism has nothing to do with the faith of those who shared Julian's or Proclus' religious beliefs, nor with the ancient civic or imperial cults that such people dreamed of restoring.

· 1 ·

What Is a Pagan?

T̲HE word "pagan," which recurs continuously throughout this book, in essence represents two ancient words: the Greek *Hellene*, and the Latin *paganus*. "Hellene" in the sense of "pagan" was as widely used by "upholders of the ancient religion" as by their adversaries, with the occasional qualification of "in matters of faith." This term is deceptive, for in the mouths of Christians it seems to include in the same censure both paganism and Greco-Roman culture, whereas long before the fifth century both Christians and pagans admired and studied the same classical texts. As a matter of fact, the term Hellene had primarily negative implications: pagans were no longer "Romans," the legitimate heirs of the Empire. And *paganus*, the root of "pagan" as well as "peasant," is consistently pejorative and poses a curious semantic problem. As it turns out, the best documented meaning of *paganus* seems to be "peasant." Urban Hellenes in the East would therefore have had country people as their counterparts in the West, which would indicate two separate evolutions.

It does not seem likely, however, that cities were Christianized more rapidly in the Western Empire than in the Eastern

Empire. The Roman Senate, a highly aristocratic assembly, counted among its members numerous pagans up to the end of the fourth century, long after the term *paganus*, in its religious meaning, had entered the legal vocabulary. There was also no dearth of pagan intellectuals in the West.[1] What is true is that in the West, Christianity remained for a longer time a religion of foreigners. At the end of the second century in Lyons, the local church was still predominantly made up of Easterners whose language was Greek. Greek was also the language of papal epitaphs in Rome in the third century.[2]

In view of this, in 1899 a German scholar, Theodore Zahn—following Denys Godefroy, the sixteenth-century commentator on the Theodosian Code—proposed starting from another meaning of *paganus*, "civilian" as opposed to "military," since Christians in third-century apologetics were often referred to as "the soldiers of Christ." Unfortunately, this metaphor, which belongs to literary or at least to elegant language, fell into disuse shortly before *paganus* entered common usage in the sense of pagan. Moreover, if there was in Late Antiquity a religion with a military bent it was Mithraism far more than Christianity.[3]

To solve the dilemma of an indisputable phonetic evolution but an incomprehensible semantic one, one must ask how the same word can have three meanings as varied as "peasant," "civilian," and "pagan." I shall begin with the first two, which are also the oldest. A *paganus* is the inhabitant of a *pagus*, a country district, a man whose roots, unlike a soldier's, are where he lives. A peasant is thus the *paganus* par excellence, although the term, from Cicero on, could denote townspeople (*Pro Domo*, 74). If one takes that factor into account, strange locutions become clear. When the poet Persius, out of genuine or false modesty, calls himself a *semipaganus* in poetry, he implies that he is only a partial member of the fraternity of poets (prologue to the *Satires*, v. 6). And when a father, on his daughter's epitaph, praises her for having been "faithful among the faithful, *pagana* among *pagani,*" he does not mean that she proselytized with paganism, but that she remained faithful to her origins.[4]

Pagani or pagans are quite simply "people of the place," town or country, who preserved their local customs, whereas the *alieni,* the "people from elsewhere," were increasingly Christian. This explanation was proposed by another Godefroy, Jacques, at the beginning of the seventeenth century, and corresponds to the etymology of the word, referred to by Christian writers who used it in its new meaning.[5] It also fits the predilection of pagans in Late Antiquity for everything that belonged to the legacy of their ancestors, *patria* in Greek. It defines paganism as a religion of the homeland in its narrowest sense: the city and its outlying countryside. And it predicts the diversity of pagan practices and beliefs.

In some cases the entrenchment of those beliefs was accompanied by a sophisticated metaphysics. For Proclus as for Ibn Arabi, "sites have an effect on sensitive hearts."[6]

This book is designed to facilitate the discovery of the "last pagans," to provide the necessary background for an encounter with them, in their works or in the historical works of their contemporaries, and to give a general account of their history, retracing the gradual loss of political power, the exclusion, the assimilation, and ultimately—however painful the term and the reality it expresses—their physical elimination. I am taking into account only indigenous polytheistic paganism, and excluding other beliefs, Manicheanism, Gnosticism, and so on, which never enjoyed political legitimacy within the framework of the Roman Empire.

Pagans Confronting the Law

Throughout Antiquity "paganism" was a mosaic of established religions linked to the political order. To be pious was "to believe in the gods of the city-state"—the duty Socrates was accused of failing to observe—and, even more than believing in them, respecting them. Ritual was thus more important than faith. Nonconformism and irreligiosity went together. From 312 on, all through the fourth century after Constantine's conversion, the state progressively rejected the ancient cults while preserving order, "without mobs or uprisings" (*sine turba ac tumultu*), as is stated in a law, and conciliating nonbelievers if they were good taxpayers, as will be seen concerning the devotees of the god Marnas in Gaza. The Christian emperors began by allowing pagan festivals to continue but prohibited their rituals. Loss of political power does not always entail decline. It is not necessarily detrimental to spirituality for a religion to detach itself from secular matters. The pagans' stubborn refusal to change religion led them, not always knowingly, to change their religion.

During the fourth century the pagans could envision an alternative to Christianity: the Sun or the Savior. At the end of the century, after Julian failed to restore paganism, the alternative was no longer an option. Only then did the ancient cults lose all official support, and not long afterward they were strictly forbidden, in theory, by the edicts of Theodosius I (392). That was not enough to make them disappear, but from then on their defenders had little more to offer than private values: with wisdom permitted and magic prohibited, the former allowed the knowledgeable use of the latter. Did those laws really affect the society they were intended to rule? As the cynic would have it, they "proved very little except that the abuses they were supposed to rectify were known to the central government."[7] Although this is only a quip and the inefficacy of Roman laws should not be exaggerated, it is true that the government doubtless had great difficulty imposing their immediate and total application. Scattered throughout the Empire, pagan communities survived locally throughout the fifth and sixth centuries, in ways that often escape us, with a dynamism and intellectual vitality that were greater in the East than in the West. Adherents were excluded from political, administrative, and military power but not from civil office or teaching, and they provided good Christian society with practitioners of "occult" sciences.

When freedom of conscience disappeared under Justinian, pagans chose either a dangerous but exciting clandestine existence that promised the manifestation of supernatural powers or else a withdrawal to hinterlands as far removed as possible from the eyes of imperial authority. Justinian's ruling of 529 that prohibited pagans from teaching shuttered the last window that enabled us to see them clearly. From then on their existence can be glimpsed only during periods of forced conversion. The single exception is a Platonic school, at Harran in Upper Mesopotamia, which survived after the Arab conquest until the arrival of the Seljuk Turks in the eleventh century, as has recently been shown by Michel Tardieu. Islam, by redrawing the political map and permanently destroying the system of the *polis*, which was replaced by another form of urban civilization, erased nearly all vestiges of the paganism of classical Antiquity.

The history that follows is therefore a kind of parallel history which cannot possibly convey in all their amplitude the great political events and theological disputes of this tumultuous period. Some of these events are mentioned incidentally, without relation to their true significance (such as the draining struggle with the Persians, because it makes all the more regrettable the destruction of a temple-citadel on the frontier), others not at all.[8] During this period pagans were not the only ones persecuted for their faith, nor was theirs the most brutal persecution; Gnostics, Manichaeans, Jews, and of course Christian heretics came in for their share as well. But only the pagans had always been intimately associated with the power and culture that dominated the Greco-Roman world. Their decline, beyond the human dramas that it engendered, was a political, intellectual, and religious revolution.

To help understand this revolution, we have at our disposal

documents whose abundance and variety are unique in all of Antiquity: accounts by historians or participants in the events seen from various sides; official acts, legal texts, inscriptions, correspondence, autobiographies, and biographies. To this can be added, on the one hand, the antipagan polemics of Christian apologists and, on the other, the pagans' own expression of their beliefs, such as hymns to the gods by the philosopher Proclus, or Orphic fragments and, though little seen from that angle, the *Dionysiaca* by the poet Nonnus of Panopolis, and the *Argonautica* in which an anonymous writer makes Orpheus the narrator. There is even a request for divorce from Horapollo, a famous pagan of the fifth century! But for the most part, this wealth of documentation is not a matter of chance. Later generations of literati, and in the East particularly, the Byzantines of the tenth-century renaissance, were aware of the importance of this period. They read, summarized, and catalogued relevant texts. The *Extracts* of Emperor Constantine VII Porphyrogenitus, the *Library* of the patriarch Photius, or the massive dictionary, the collective work titled *Souda*, all contain precious information about the men and works of those times.

In spite of these favorable conditions, enormous gaps force the researcher to utilize all available information without always being certain of its importance. Even so, ancient history remains wholly refractory to quantitative evaluations, and certain judgments rest on foundations that are far from solid because the passions of religious controversy, for or against Christianity, are nowhere near extinguished even today. Another passion has been more discreet, for it remained restricted to the world of scholarship, but it too has played havoc with our perception of the Antique world: a "hypercritical" attitude that often has precluded the understanding and use of texts considered wholly or partially spurious, or garbled accounts that the scholar had to correct in order to restore to the event its lost logic. Such was the case with two works as different as the *Life of Constantine* by Bishop Eusebius or the *Life of Porphyry* by Marcus the Deacon. They provide valuable evidence, but it must be kept in mind that they are apologies, not "objective" narratives.[9] All things considered, though so much has already been written on this turning point of world history, there is justification for returning to the facts, as honestly as possible.

· 2 ·

An Empire in Search
of Religion

IT should be a truism to say
that in 312, when Christianity in virtually one fell swoop
gained permanent rights of existence and, being the emper-
or's religion, the privileges of a state religion, it was not a
"new" religion. But actually it is not, for opponents who accused it of abandoning ancestral traditions are responsible for
giving it the image of a revolutionary movement. By 312, the
Christians had long been integrated into Roman society, par-
ticipating in its culture and its entertainments. The accounts
of the martyrdoms of Perpetua in Carthage (in 203) and of
Pionius in Smyrna (in 250) demonstrate that Christian faithful
were familiar with the athletic and musical contests that their
contemporaries enjoyed; they naturally borrow images from
them to depict the final test that athletes of God must over-
come before Christ grants them victory.[1] In the realm of spiritual matters, third-century Alexandria witnessed the flower-
ing of Christian Platonists, Clement and Origen among
others. A man by the name of Anatolius, who started a school
of Aristotelian philosophy in that city, became bishop of
Laodicea in 269. In Africa, Tertullian, and later Arnobius and

his pupil Lactantius, prove that Christians were at home in classical culture.[2]

Either shortly after 300, or perhaps in May 309, an assembly of bishops met in Illiberis (Elvira), in Spain, to tell the faithful what was permitted and what was not. In other words, a council established "disciplinary canons."Although the precise date of this assembly is not certain, it is clear from its concerns that it was legislating for "normal" conditions, when Christians were free from harassment—thus not during the years 303–305—but when public life was dominated by official paganism. Under discussion was the matter of Christian ladies' lending their fine robes to a neighbor for pagan holidays, of Christian masters feeling obliged to let their slaves worship idols and being sometimes tempted themselves to seek the favors of those same idols. As often happens, the rules established by defining infractions give glimpses of private life, less sinful to us today than in the eyes of the stern bishops who met in Illiberis.

Among the problems they had to resolve was that of Christians who were raised to local positions of honor such as that of *duumvir*, one of the two presidents of the municipal council, or *flamen*, a priest of the imperial cult. The prestige of the office was related to the holder's generosity. At the time of his nomination, he was expected to make a bequest to the municipal treasury as well as a gift to the people and, later, to provide his fellow citizens with entertainments—plays or gladiatorial contests. He also had to preside over ceremonies that we would consider religious, or at least be present at them.

The bishops decided that as long as *duumvirs* held office they should not attend Christian services, and that *flamines* who had made pagan sacrifices should be permanently excluded from the Church. Those who had offered spectacles would be treated as adulterers (because of the immorality of the theater) or murderers (because of the gladiators). Those who had merely worn the obligatory crown in such ceremonies would be readmitted to the Church after two years.

These are rigorous measures. In 314 the Council of Arles decided that governors, and in general "those who wish to concern themselves with public affairs" (*hi qui rem publicam agere volunt*), would still be admitted to communion on the recommendation of their bishop. Much later, in 525, in Africa, then under Vandal domination, people called "perpetual *flamines*" were buried in Christian basilicas. What did such a title mean at that time? The reason it managed to survive is that it had ceased to have any more than a social meaning.[3] But even before the Council of Elvira, the spread of Christianity had not been limited to the gentry of small towns, in Spain or elsewhere. Diocletian's persecutions in 303 revealed the Christian sympathies or beliefs of the emperor's wife and daughter and some of their personal servants; of Adauctus, a high treasury official, as well as the director of the purple dye factories in Tyre, the eunuch Dorotheus,[4] and others.

Christians, whose religious message included a new, broader, and more generous kind of solidarity—which Momigliano calls "a new commonwealth of men for men"—were no longer a small semiclandestine marginal group.[5] Around 180 the Platonic philosopher Celsus could still joke while attacking them: "If all men wanted to be Christians, Christians would not want them." In 248, under the pro-Christian reign of Philip the Arab, Origen contradicts him, exclaiming: "Though there are no workers to bring in the harvest of souls, there is such a great harvest of men brought in and gathered together on the threshing-floors of God, the churches, which are everywhere!"[6] Moreover, Celsus, even while speaking ironically of the elitism of Christians, acknowledges the spread of their religion, which Origen confirms: among them are rich people, high officials, elegant, well-born ladies. It is not possible to be more precise, since the term both writers use, "multitude" (*plethos*), is highly subjective. Only for certain parts of Egypt was the papyrologist Roger Bagnall able to trace a curve of growth more rapid and earlier than had been thought.[7]

The third century was the century of persecutions—in fact the only persecutions inflicted on Christianity generally. They took place during the great crisis that shook the Roman Empire: first under Decius, beginning in February 250, after a period of support in the reign of Philip the Arab (244–249), and lasting until the death of that emperor (at the end of June 251), who had added the name of Trajan to that of Decius in order to indicate his determination to restore the Empire; then under Valerian, from 257 until his fall in June 260, when he was taken prisoner by the Persians; and finally under Diocletian, the reorganizer, who ascended the throne in November 284. On February 23, 303, at the end of eighteen years of rule and at the height of his power, Diocletian outlawed Christianity. After his abdication two years later, the persecutions he had initiated continued for another seven years under some of his successors, notably Galerius and Maximinus Daia in the East.

What was the nature of these persecutions? Under Decius, all inhabitants of the Empire were required to sacrifice to the gods, to pour libations, and to eat the sacrificial meat; those who refused could be sentenced to death. The enforcement of this order led a large number of Christians into apostasy, particularly the well-to-do, sometimes even bishops, as in Smyrna (*Acts of Pionius*); others rejoined the synagogue. Once the danger had passed, many of those who had given in to the pressure, "lapsed" Christians (*lapsi*), sought to reenter the fold; this resulted in discussions of the conditions for their pardon. Under Valerian, it was the wealth of the Church that interested the state, so that at first enforcement was directed only at the clergy (August 257). Later (in the summer of 258), it was extended to include prominent lay persons. The proceedings were skeletal at times, as indicated by a hearing conducted by a governor in Spain:

"You are a bishop?"
"I am."
"You were."

And he sentenced him to be burned alive. (*Episcopus es?* —*Sum*. —*Fuisti*. Acts of Fructuosus, 2.)

Under Diocletian, the Manichaeans were outlawed first, on 31 March 297. Their doctrine came from Persia and the Empire was at war with Persia.[8] Books and priests were to be seized and burned; most believers were put to death with dispatch. The lives of prominent citizens, *honestiores*, were spared, but their goods were confiscated and they were sent to work in the mines. Six years later, after having consulted the oracle of Apollo at Didyma, Diocletian published his first decree against Christians, issued on 23 February 303, the day of the Roman festival of *Terminalia*, a fortunate date for those who wished to "terminate" the impiety.[9] Their churches were to be destroyed, their sacred books burned. Christian *honestiores* were removed from office, and Christian slaves could not be freed. The community at large lost its civil rights; the testimony of its members was inadmissible in crimes against individuals (assault, adultery, theft); and they were excluded from all public employment. Christians were probably too numerous by then to be exterminated by the emperor, but he hoped at least to destroy their power and their wealth.

The unhesitating resistance of believers—who, as we have seen, were to be found even within Diocletian's closest circle—provoked in him a virulent response to what he considered defiance of his authority. Executions increased. Disorders may have triggered attempts on the throne in which Christians were not necessarily implicated. Insurgents appeared in Melitene (today's basin of Malatya on the Upper Euphrates in eastern Turkey) and in Syria, from the harbor of Seleucia, where a shortage of corn provoked a mutiny in an engineering force, to Antioch, capital of the province. The grandfather and granduncle of the orator Libanius, both pagan squires and members of the local council at Antioch, were put to death along with many others; insurgent areas were subjected to a fierce repression.[10] Such troubles gave Diocletian grounds to issue new edicts, worse than the first. During the summer of 303 one went out to all Christian clergy ordering them to sacrifice to the gods under pain of imprisonment. In the first months of 304 this order was extended to the entire population, collectively, in each city. In this manner, the Augustus Diocletian and his attendant, the Caesar Galerius, compelled demonstrations of loyalty toward their rough and perhaps not very popular rule.

Diocletian, whose health was failing, abdicated on May 1, 305. His successors in the East—the new Augustus, Galerius, and his nephew, the new Caesar, Maximinus Daia—were the only ones to continue the persecutions energetically. But even they had to abnegate them some time before their death or their fall. Galerius, grievously ill and realizing that power was slipping out of his hands, issued an edict of tolerance on April 30, 311. He died one week later. Maximinus too, near the end of his reign (from the end of 312 on), had to reconcile himself to such a policy. This probably did not prevent some local harassment in his dominion before his defeat on April 30, 313.

Diocletian's coemperor for the West, the Augustus Maximian, enforced only the first edict; his adjutant in Gaul, the Caesar Constantius, limited himself to demolishing a few churches. As for the governors, it depended on their personal idiosyncrasies. The governor of Byzacium (in the region of Sousse, Tunisia) was rather mild as a persecutor, while those of Africa and Numidia were active enforcers of the law. As a rule, they confiscated the books and holdings of the Church, but refrained from harming believers and the clergy, less for humanitarian reasons than to avoid uprisings, which nevertheless broke out violently in Egypt and Palestine. It is difficult for us to appreciate how tight the net that persecutors were endeavoring to draw around their subjects actually was. In Egypt, the Christian historian Eusebius of Caesarea describes the faithful of Thebais rushing to martyrdom, but in a document from Oxyrhynchus, farther down the Nile Valley, we learn that Christians anxious to avoid the compulsory offering of a sacrifice could, in a legal hearing, empower a third party—in that instance, the brother of the man concerned—to act in their behalf.[11] We may wonder whether this brother had previously remained pagan while his family was turning to Christianity, or whether he had been chosen by some family council to apostasize and represent its members in such official acts.

The people themselves were little inclined to collaborate in the persecutions, except in a few places, like Gaza, which long remained a pagan city.[12] During the winter or early spring of 311–312, large cities like Tyre, Antioch, Nicomedia, the province (*ethnos*) of Lycia-Pamphylia, or lesser communities like the city of Colbasa in Pisidia, sent petitions against the Christians to Maximinus, perhaps solicited in some cases (as Eusebius and Lactantius assert, and as the uniformity of the imperial responses would indicate).[13] In his reply (rescript) to Colbasa, delivered in Sardis on April 6, 312, the emperor seems to promise some exemption from the very unpopular poll tax. But whatever pressure may have been exerted by imperial agents, whatever inducements may have been offered, these petitions were not fake. Apart from Antioch, the signatories, whether cities or regions, maintained their commitment to paganism until much later.

Maximinus Daia, as W. H. C. Frend has remarked, was "the most intelligent of the persecutors," and the only one before Julian to have tried to reconvert Christians.[14] His attempt to involve the people in his struggle, noted by Eusebius and Lactantius, was also his innovation. It is no longer believed today that cultic associations, like the Xenoi Tecmoreioi at Antioch in Pisidia, were founded by the emperors at an earlier date to halt the progress of Christianity in their realms.[15]

These persecutions engendered schisms and gave rise to Arianism, a heresy whose fate would not be decided until the reign of Theodosius II, at the end of the fourth century. But they also led the Church to endow itself with a solid administrative structure and did not weaken it in any lasting way. While one may argue over the number of victims in these persecutions, they represent a mere handful of the total number of believers. This was perceived as early as the end of the seventeenth century, with the ground-breaking dissertation by Dodwell, "About the Small Number of Martyrs" (*De paucitate martyrum*).[16]

What were the perpetrators, otherwise excellent rulers, trying to achieve through these persecutions? Theirs were the only ones to be systematic, although there were other waves of intolerance, such as that under Aurelian (270–275). Essentially, their goal was the unity of the Empire. In 212 Caracalla granted Roman citizenship to all free inhabitants (*Constitutio Antoniniana*). All citizens were therefore expected to participate in the cults of the immense city that the Empire had become. They began by obeying, and under Decius there is no indication of laxity on the part of magistrates appointed to enforce the law, nor any popular movement to protect Christians. From that moment there was a state religion, not merely a multitude of civil cults to which was added, halfway between religion and politics, the cult of the emperor. The person of the emperor was now exalted, consecrated as never before. Diocletian placed himself as "Augustus" and his adjutant Galerius as "Caesar" under the special protection of Jupiter, while his coemperor the "Augustus" Maximian, along with his "Caesar," Constantius, were to invoke Hercules. Tradition provided the basis for a uniformity that was presented as a restoration.

The motivation for the persecutions in the third century is the same as that which, in the next century, sealed an alliance of throne and altar—an alliance that was to have such a brilliant future. Because of these upheavals, Christians ceased being a subversive group awaiting the end of the world and the apocalypse, or at least ceased appearing as such. A more optimistic view of man's destiny and his place in the world was adopted by the Church. The secular power with all its gorgeous celebrations was by then a servant of the faith, indistinguishable from it. At the beginning of the fourth century bishops admitted to Constantine's presence fancied him to be a "Lord's angel" and the majesty of his throne to be "a picture of Christ's kingship." [17]

· 3 ·

Constantine's Christian Empire

THE Christian Empire was
Constantine's creation, but its religious evolution was complex. For our purposes, it began in 310 in the midst of the
confusion over the imperial succession. After Diocletian's re-
forms of 286 and 293, the throne provided four posts to whet
the appetites of pretenders. By then the supreme rulers were
two, bearing the title of Augusti, one for the West and one for
the East. (The first were Diocletian and Maximian.) Each was
flanked by one Caesar, his adjutant and presumptive heir,
generally impatient to succeed him. There was a religious
side to this reorganization: Diocletian placed himself under
the patronage of Jupiter, his co-Augustus Maximian invoking
Hercules, which clearly suggests a hierarchical order. The relation between Caesar and Augustus was a fictitious filiation,
according to a method of adoption between adults that seems
very artificial today but was a commonplace to Romans.

In this complex structure of the tetrarchy Constantius I,
Constantine's father, was at that time Maximian's Caesar, in
the "Herculean" line. In 305 Diocletian decided that both Augusti should abdicate, and Maximian was obliged to defer to
him. Constantius consequently became Augustus. But it was

only after the death of his father that Constantine, on his own initiative, proclaimed himself Caesar (306), then Augustus in 307. Although he had the title, it was necessary for him to enforce his authority. Toward this end the celestial powers offered a helping hand. In 310 Constantine had a vision in one of the sanctuaries of Apollo in Gaul, perhaps at Grand, in the Vosges. The Sun God appeared to him, accompanied by Victory, presenting him with laurel crowns on each of which was inscribed the sign for the number thirty—three X's—thus promising a life—and reign—of exceptional length.[1]

Until then Constantine had been basing the legitimacy of his power on his relation with the Herculean dynasty of Maximian. Maximian was both his adoptive (fictitious) grandfather, thanks to Constantius, and his actual father-in-law. After the prophetic event in Gaul, Constantine fostered the cult of the Sun God instead of that of Hercules, thereby associating himself with the dynasty that god had protected, that of Claudius Gothicus (268–270), victor over the Alamanni and the Goths, who had chosen as his successor Aurelian (270–275), promoter of the official cult of the Unconquerable Sun. Constantine, whose father, like Claudius, was a Dalmatian, claimed descent from that emperor. After all, was not the great Augustus himself, founder of the Principate, already a devotee of Apollo? Of all the gods, the truest and most genuine champion of Rome was ostensibly taking sides with the new self-proclaimed Augustus.

Constantine captured Maximian in Marseilles and had him put to death (or forced to commit suicide) in May 311. He then sought the support of the Christians against his rival, Maxentius, Maximian's son, who was defeated and killed on October 28, 312, at the battle near the Milvian bridge, at the gates of Rome. Like Apollo in 310, the god of the Christians sent him, before the battle, a sign of his favor. Two divergent and equally authoritative accounts of the precise nature of this apparition have come down to us from two of the emperor's associates, Lactantius and Eusebius.

Lactantius wrote *On the Death of the Persecutors* (meaning those emperors who persecuted Christians) in the West in 314–315, not long after the actual event. He placed the vision at night, just before the battle at the Milvian bridge. Lactantius more than likely heard about this from Constantine himself, with whom he was already in favor. (Before 317 he was named tutor in Latin literature to the emperor's elder son, Crispus.)[2] In the dream Constantine was instructed to place on his soldiers' shields the monogram of Christ.[3]

The second witness, Eusebius, wrote only after Constantine's death (337), but he had met him several times and claimed to be relating personal confidences. The emperor, on his way to overthrow Maxentius but perhaps still in Gaul, is said to have seen in the sky, just past midday, the glowing sign of the cross with the inscription "Conquer with this" (rendered in Greek by Eusebius). The next night a dream told him to use this sign for protection.[4] This account contains the same elements as the Apollonian vision: the sun, X's or a cross, victory. It is explained by a dream that reminds us vividly of the dream before the battle of the Milvian bridge, which led Constantine to use Christ's monogram as a military insignia. This might be considered a reinterpretation of the Apollonian miracle and the Christian dream, combining their virtues in a unique episode. Such an arrangement could have been devised by the emperor himself, not necessarily as a trick, when, near the end of his life, he had completely renounced his devotion to the Sun.[5]

In February 313, at Milan, Constantine and Licinius, his colleague for the East, enacted an edict that Licinius, once Maximinus had been overthrown in April, posted in Nicomedia on June 13. This edict allows freedom for all religious beliefs, giving the Christian faith a privileged but not exclusive place.[6]

We resolved to grant Christians and all other men freedom to observe whatever religion they think fit, so that the divinity, who has his abode in heaven, be propitious and benevolent as well for us as for any of those living under our rule. It seemed to us a very good and very reasonable system to refuse to none of our subjects, whether a Christian or a follower of some other cult, the right to observe the religion that suits him best . . . We leave Christians the fullest and the most absolute freedom to celebrate their cult; and, as we grant Christians that right . . . other people also must enjoy it. It is fit for the era we live in, it suits the peace which benefits the Empire, that full freedom be given to all our subjects to worship the god they elected, and that no cult be deprived of due honors.

These lines opened an era that would be finally closed only with Justinian.

Actually, Christian emblems appear on Constantine's coins perhaps as early as 313 or at the latest 315, in striking conjunction with his portrait as conquering warrior: to the left of the imperial bust, helmeted and cuirassed, is a cross surmounted by a globe; the helmet bears the monogram of Christ; to the right is the head of a horse. Nevertheless, until 317, and again as late as 325, three-fourths of the coins minted by Constantine continued to be dedicated to "the Unconquerable Sun, his companion," *Soli Invicto Comiti*, while Christian symbols occasionally appear on the reverse.[7] Whatever the innermost convictions of the emperor—during the years between his victories over Maxentius (312) and Licinius (324), his last colleague and competitor, he may have been mainly convinced of his divine right to supreme power—he found it convenient to pay his respects to both Christ and Apollo and to make use of Apollonian imagery, perhaps not merely for political purposes.

On the Arch of Constantine in Rome, which commemorates his 312 triumph, it is neither Jupiter, the old conventional patron of Rome, nor Christ, already the quasi-official Savior, but Apollo the Sun God who is in the foreground, as the god of the army and of the prince. The inscription on the arch, as ecumenical as anyone could wish, attributes the victory to "the inspiration of the divinity," *instinctu divinitatis*, and, equally important, to the ruler's noble soul.[8]

The scales were thus approximately balanced. A law of 321 institutes as a day of rest Sunday, "the day of the sun," whose name has remained quite explicit in English (*dies solis veneratione sua celebris*, Theodosian Code, II, 8, 1). It is also for Christians "the day of the Lord"—when He was resurrected (*dies dominica* in Latin, whence Italian *domenica* and, less obvious, French *dimanche*). This institution of the week as an official division of time, with its dual reference—planetary and solar on the one hand, sabbatic on the other—played an important role at the end of the century, when the law prohibited pagan cults and holidays associated with them, and proclaimed the Christianization of the calendar as well as of the rhythm of daily life.[9]

Constantinople, City of the Sun?

In 324, after eliminating Licinius, who reigned over the East, Constantine became sole master of the Empire. The same year he decided to "found" Constantinople, which was inaugurated six years later, on May 11, 330. The term "found" does not mean a creation *ex nihilo*. An ancient and already important city, Byzantium, received a new name. At the same time its urban center was renovated for new functions. Unlike other large Eastern cities that it would eclipse, Constantinople from the outset was a city whose inhabitants were increasingly Christians and in which churches outnumbered temples, as Libanius acknowledged at the end of the century.[10] Constantine, who during this same period presided over the Council of Nicaea (325) and seized every opportunity to display consideration toward the bishops, giving them official means of travel and entertaining them at banquets, had long since espoused Christianity, but chose to retain a certain number of solar symbols for their political value, especially since many were not incompatible with Christianity. Christ was commonly characterized as the Light of the World, *Lux Mundi* in Latin, and Sun of Justice, *Helios Dikaiosynes* in Greek. As Cyril Mango points out, around 328 Constantine had himself portrayed in his capital, on the top of a porphyry column, wearing the radiate crown of the Sun God. He went even farther, by having a Capitol constructed in the city, that is, a temple dedicated to the triad Jupiter-Juno-Minerva, and the "essential symbol of Romanness." [11]

The political significance is all the clearer in that Constantine was completely indifferent to Jupiter. In Rome he refused to go to the Capitol to make a sacrifice. His refusal was probably motivated by aversion to the offering of blood sacrifice, which was reminiscent of the persecutions of Christians. Allegedly, his failure almost cost him his popularity in Rome, a city that remained faithful to ancestral rites. This information, however, comes from a pagan historian who was writing almost two centuries after Constantine's reign, at a time when paganism had been stamped out, and who does not conceal his resentment toward the founder of the Christian Empire (Zosimus, II, 29, 5). (Forty years later Julian made himself unpopular in Christianized Antioch for the exact opposite reason: too many rituals and sacrifices, not enough amusements.) When Constantine was founding his capital, he hired the services of a hierophant, a certain Praetextatus, and a *telestes* (initiate), Sopater of Apamea, a Neoplatonic philosopher and disciple of Iamblichus, thereby conforming to the most classical of traditions. [12]

Even when the emperor appropriated the statues and exvotos of the great sanctuaries to decorate his city—as had many of his predecessors, including Nero—a pagan political-religious intention can still be discerned in certain cases. According to Zosimus, a watchful witness for that sort of thing, Constantine took from Cyzicus a very ancient wooden statue of Cybele, said to have been consecrated by the Argonauts, and had it placed under a portico facing the figure of the Roman Tyche, so that she seemed to be gazing out at and watching over the city. The statue was modified slightly: the lions that stood on either side were eliminated, and Cybele's hands were rearranged in a gesture that came to mean prayer (palms facing outward). A nineteenth-century German scholar, W. Amelung, admirably explained this modification: a statue of Cybele, main goddess of Asia Minor, as "Mistress of the Animals" (taming or gripping wild beasts), dating from the seventh or sixth century B.C., had been transformed into a representation of Tyche, the Fortuna of Constantinople, and placed opposite the Fortuna of Rome. Cybele's turreted crown suited this role, as did the modification of her hands, so that the new city saw itself endowed with a protector both new and venerable, alluding for the literati to the visit paid by the Argonauts to the sites of Cyzicus and Byzantium, at the dawn of history.[13] The statue was not changed into a praying figure, and we must not make false inferences from Zosimus' text.[14] This historian was simply using a comparison to explain the position of the hands, not their meaning, which actually is protective here.

The same intention of exploiting for his own purposes the magical power of ancient statues can be seen in Constantine's decision to use for the representation of the emperor on the top of his porphyry column a statue of Apollo from Ilium (Troy), whose head was recarved for the occasion. Apollo had been the great defender of Troy (whose heir, via Aeneas, Rome considered itself); and as the Sun God, he protected Constantine. Similarly, the *palladion* was transferred from Rome to Constantinople. This relic, said to have been brought to Italy from Troy by Aeneas, was a very old statue of Athena, which made impregnable any city that possessed it.[15]

The emperor may not himself have selected these pagan symbols of enduring power, but he did agree to strip other cities for the purpose of decorating Constantinople. At that time those in charge of the renovations probably were pagans.[16] Bishop Eusebius, evidently embarrassed, maintained that this display of antiquities and works of art was intended to discredit the old beliefs. Although such an intention has been documented for a later date, the number and quality of the statues involved in the renovation of Constantine's city, as well as the place assigned to them, make it unlikely that this was Constantine's motive.

Constantine's Pragmatism

Constantine's legislation with regard to paganism only renewed measures that went back to Tiberius and were motivated by political rather than religious considerations. Such was his prohibition against sacrifices (religious slaughtering) and divination (from the victim's entrails or otherwise) within private dwellings. For the rest, the emperor told his subjects: "go to the altars and public sanctuaries and accomplish the rites you customarily observe."[17] Plato had already condemned private cults, to prevent worshipers from offering sacrifices in a state of impurity: "they believe that they can secretly gain the favor of the gods through sacrifices and prayers" (*Laws*, X end, 909a-910d). The old Roman law echoed Plato's voice, forbidding the worship of "new or foreign gods, unless they have been officially accepted" (Cicero, *De Legibus*, II, 8). During the fourth century the former gods became increasingly more foreign to the emperors and to their subjects. By the end of the century, when these gods had lost all official recognition, their cult was on the eve of being strictly prohibited. But that did not occur until 383 and thereafter. Constantine's laws did not aim at reducing paganism, but at controlling the exercise of powers (divination and magic) held by certain priests. A distinction is made between licit magic, for health and harvests, and illicit magic, to bring about someone's death or seduction.[18] Public consultations of soothsayers were allowed if lightning fell on the palace or on public buildings.[19] These stipulations, in fact, echo the law of the Twelve Tables and legislation of the High Empire.[20] The Constantinian wording is much more subtle than his panegyrist, Eusebius, who was eager to picture his hero as an uncompromising champion of Christ, would have us believe (*Life of Constantine*, II, 44).

Two examples illustrate Constantine's pragmatism in matters of religion. Both cases concern actions taken on behalf of cities that sought to be free from the domination of a more important neighbor. In Phrygia, the small city of Orcistus had been annexed by its neighbor Nacoleia around 260, under Gallienus, and so demoted from the rank of city, *polis*, to borough, *kômê*. So Nacoleia, extending its territory southeast, along the right bank of the Sangarius, acquired a fertile country, where abundant waters worked mills to grind corn and roads of some importance crossed. Around 325 the inhabitants of Orcistus petitioned for the return of their independence. Constantine accorded them all the rights of a duly constituted city; moreover, in recognition of the fact that all the inhabitants were "believers in the very holy religion," he dispensed them from paying taxes for the pagan cults. Nacoleia, the rival city, maintained its paganism, as can be seen from a much later inscription honoring Julian. In 331 Orcistus had to send a new petition to Constantine, as Nacoleia solicited contributions for the cults.[21]

In 333 the inhabitants of Hispellum in Umbria asked permission of Constantine, emperor of the Flavian dynasty, to rename their city Flavia Constans, to build a temple to the imperial family there, and to give performances of plays and hold gladiatorial contests in his honor. Constantine willingly accepted their offer, on condition that the new cult did not include blood sacrifices. The inhabitants of Hispellum agreed to the restriction. Their main objective—dictated by convenience as much as local pride—had been to avoid subsidizing the festivals of their neighbor, Volsiniae, every other year. In Rome, Constantine would also have prohibited sacrifices during public games, but not under other circumstances.[22]

Constantine recognized a most unusual feature of Christianity: its exclusivity. In 323 he ruled against requiring Christians to sacrifice; he also ruled against their voluntary participation in the sacrifices.[23] It is in this context that a pagan sanctuary in Mambre (in Judaea, near Hebron) was destroyed: the oak under which the three angels of God, or rather God Himself accompanied by two angels, appeared to Abraham was the object of a cult, like many other sacred trees, for pagans as well as Jews and Christians. Constantine ordered the pagan altar to be razed to the ground and the idols that profaned the place to be burned.[24]

Morality

An outstanding example of those cults that were effectively stamped out by the emperor is that of the temple of Aphrodite in Aphaca, now Efqa, in Lebanon, an enchanting site near the springs of Adonis. Transvestites as well as women prostituted themselves there, and Constantine had the temple razed.[25] The site has remained no less sacred down to the present. In Heliopolis (Baalbek), also in Phoenicia, where apparently only women prostituted themselves in veneration of Aphrodite, Constantine limited himself to urging greater restraint on the population and to building a church. Heliopolis nonetheless remained pagan for more than two centuries after that, and it took a military expedition at the end of the sixth century to Christianize the Bekaa. In Egypt, Constantine prohibited the castration of priests of the Nile, but allowed the continuation of ceremonies and festivals to encourage the flooding of the river.[26]

The emperor's concerns seem at first glance to be moral rather than specifically Christian. (Certain fervent pagans preached chastity and even abstinence, from Porphyry to Julian and beyond.)[27] Severity toward homosexuality is a mark of the time. Opposition to sexual mutilations was an old Roman tradition: the pagan historian Ammianus Marcellinus praised Domitian's law on the subject. This can be compared with the attitude of King Abgar of Edessa (177–212), who is said to have prohibited self-castration in his realm, although it was a practice associated with the cult of the goddess of Hierapolis Manbiğ. It is uncertain whether this king, who was friendly to Christians, was himself a Christian.[28] All this remains somewhat ambiguous, if one may say so given the context, since the emperors of the Late Empire employed the services of eunuchs, and sometimes their bodies when they were attractive. The contradiction between the general rule and the private practice of a ruler can also be seen in regard to divination. And one of Constantine's sons, Constans, who himself was a homosexual, banned homosexuality on pain of death.[29]

The Attack on Asclepius

Eusebius claims that Constantine ordered the army to demolish the magnificent temple of Asclepius at Aigeai in Cilicia, one of the god's chief sanctuaries. It would seem, however, that it was the bishop of the city who, in 326, stripped the temple of its exterior colonnade in order to reuse it as the nave of a church. Julian ordered him, or rather his successor, to restore it at his own expense.[30] The Byzantine historian Zonaras reports that when the pagans tried to retrieve the columns, they were unable to get any of them through the church's portals. Miracles apart, those columns were not the most manageable; on more than one occasion we find mention of the difficulty of destroying large sanctuaries and it was no less difficult to restore them. Eusebius, in his concern to glorify his hero, the emperor, apparently attributed to him an initiative that was actually local. Fifty years later the great orator Libanius of Antioch, a city not far from Aigeai, reproached Constantine for his religious policies and bitterly regretted the destruction of the temple of Asclepius,[31] but did not blame the emperor for it. According to another personage of the region, Theodoret, bishop of Cyrhus, it was not until 386 that a bishop "used the law as a weapon for the first time" to demolish a temple (bishop Marcellus in Apamea).

What emerges, as Louis Robert has pointed out, is Eusebius' veritable hatred of Asclepius, "Savior" and "philanthropos," whom he regarded as Christ's competitor. But here as elsewhere, the destruction of the temple did not lead to the immediate disappearance of the Asclepius cult in Aigeai. We do have later evidence for it: in 355 in Epidaurus, the birthplace of the god and his main sanctuary, a priest made a dedication to the Asclepius of Aigeai. Libanius consulted him between 362 and 365. The reasons for the early destruction of so prestigious a sanctuary and the circumstances that made it possible are not entirely clear. Perhaps in his metropolis, the bishop, wishing to imitate the emperor who decorated his capital by plundering temples elsewhere, seized the occasion to humiliate a rival cult at the same time.[32] In any case, this is far below the level of organized destruction of sanctuaries that took place at the end of the century. One need only compare this limited act of vandalism with the total destruction of the temple of Zeus Marnas in Gaza.

• • •

THESE measures taken together indicate the orientation of lawmakers of later periods, up to and beyond the edicts of Theodosius: public expression of morality; rejection of bloody animal sacrifices; distrust of auguries (related to such sacrifices); occasional recourse to some seemingly harmless pagan practices ("white magic"). But above all, there was a pragmatic attitude toward spectacles and popular pleasures associated with traditional celebrations. The lawmaker respected the customs he had no power to alter, as one can see with regard to gladiatorial contests. These continued to appear on programs although Constantine, in a law of 325, became the first emperor to criticize them officially and to replace the sentencing of criminals to the games with work in the mines.[33]

· 4 ·

The Wavering Fourth Century

DURING the reign of Constantine's sons, Constans in the West (337–350) and Constantius, first in the East and later over the entire Empire (337–361), religious politics took on greater importance. At first it was a question of settling quarrels between Orthodox Christians and Arians by accepting the decisions of the Council of Nicaea, over which Constantine presided in 325. Orthodoxy did not achieve victory until some fifty years later, under Theodosius I. Constans was Orthodox and Constantius, Arian; both were born Christians. A law promulgated by Constantius in 341—during the early years of the brothers' reign, shortly after Constans had eliminated their elder brother Constantine II in 340—opens with a blustering exhortation: *Cesset superstitio, sacrificiorum aboleatur insania,* "Let superstition come to an end, and the insanity of sacrifices be abolished." But after these demands, the emperor merely repeats prohibitions already made by Constantine in 319 and 320 (Theodosian Code, XVI, 10, 2). *Superstitio* thus does not refer here to the cult of idols, but to divination through the entrails of sacrificial animals, which in no way implies a prohibition of official pagan ceremonies. Precisely in the Roman cult, Constantius retained his title of *pontifex maximus*.

A law of 342 (Theodosian Code, XVI, 10, 3) proves that pagan holidays were not under attack. It prohibits the destruction of the temples outside the walls, because some of them are associated with the origins of Rome's spectacles, circus games, and contests (*ludi, circenses, agones*), and because through their presence the Roman people can participate in "the solemnity of their ancient entertainments." This law, which J. Geffcken (p. 97) deems "unclear," evidently does not mean that destruction of temples within the city is permitted. The sanctuaries that stood isolated in open countryside or in sacred woods, sanctuaries that were rarely used or used only for certain precise occasions were more vulnerable than those in the cities. The law attempts to protect those more or less abandoned temples from plunder. It should be compared with another law dating from 349 (Theodosian Code, IX, 17, 2), directed against lime workers and dealers in used building materials. It reveals the progressive deterioration of buildings, which Julian tried to halt by launching a bold policy of restoration and reconstruction. Does this suggest a falling away of believers? Perhaps. But after more than a millennium of rituals and consecrations, after all the many political upheavals since the reign of Marcus Aurelius, there were surely many buildings that no longer corresponded to the current needs of the cult or to the distribution of inhabitants throughout the countryside, or for that matter the cities.

Constantius did not hesitate to call upon the services of eminent pagans, orators in particular. In 341, at the inauguration of the "great church" that Constantius had built in Antioch, a pagan sophist, Bemarchius, delivered the official speech in praise of the edifice. We know this from his colleague and rival Libanius, who reproached him for it. Libanius' irritation was provoked more by professional rivalry than religious scruples. At the beginning of his stay in Constantinople, he himself had offered a panegyric to Constantius, who greatly appreciated it. But far more than Bemarchius, who was a secondary figure, or than the touchy Libanius, it was Themistius who was the incarnation of the intellectual and first rank pagan civil servant attending Christian emperors from the reign of Constantius to that of Theodosius—almost the whole of the fourth century. An eloquent professor and commentator on Aristotle, he was not satisfied with delivering ceremonial speeches or, as in 357, leading the senate delegation from Constantinople that offered Constantius, then in Rome, a gold crown for his jubilee after twenty years on the throne. The following year he was proconsul of Constantinople, which amounts to being governor, a position he held again in 384 with the title of "prefect of the city of Constantinople." And around 380, some ten years before outlawing pagan cults, the very Christian Theodosius entrusted to this pagan philosopher the education of the imperial prince Arcadius, then a child of three or four. A splendid career, whose success was owed not only to the flexibility of his backbone and his facility with words, but also to his human qualities and to his abilities as a man of action.[1]

The Turning Point of 353

The first serious measures against pagan cults were taken by the imperial government after Magnentius' victory over Constans and his attempted usurpation. Magnentius had been tolerant of pagans (January 18, 350, to August 10, 353). On November 23, 353, the nocturnal sacrifices that he had authorized (Theodosian Code, XVI, 10, 5) were prohibited; a year later everyone, on pain of death, was forbidden to make any sacrifices. This led to the closing of the temples (December 1, 354; Code, XVI, 10, 4). The ruling was renewed on February 19, 356 (Code, XVI, 10, 6), and it was specified that the worship of statues was forbidden. In 357, during his visit to Rome, Constantius had the altar of Victory removed from the Senate.[2] The altar was erected in front of a statue of the goddess commemorating the victory of Constantine over Maxentius; that remained in place. Vastly impressed with the majesty of the city's monuments, the emperor assured the senators (largely pagan) of their privileges and left untouched the revenues of the temples and the traditional priesthoods (which were magistracies and not what we would consider priestly offices). Moreover, Constantius did not relinquish control over them, appointing their holders and in that respect fulfilling his duties as *pontifex maximus* of a religion that, over the centuries, one could heed without being a believer.

The years 354 to 358 were, in Geffcken's words, years of "religious fury." The laws of 357–358 proscribed sorcery and divination: soothsayers, readers of entrails, astrologers, augurers, and sorcerers were denied the right to practice. But the peremptory tone of the dictates ("let the curiosity to know the future be silenced for all forever," *sileat omnibus perpetuo divinandi curiositas*) was not enough to stifle so great a yearning, at a time when no one doubted that the art of prediction was a true science. Such a science was no more given to mistakes than painting, which, like divination, reproduced reality, or medicine, which also offered the individual a remedy for misfortune. When Libanius wished to consult the gods in secret, he asked his correspondent to contact "the doctors," but a metonymy as obvious as that fooled neither the slave who intercepted the letter nor the judge who read it.[3]

Everyone looked to the meaning of signs and to magic to explain the reason for life's little miseries and to find some relief for them—such as Libanius' headaches, whose diagnosis and treatment were accepted by doctors—or to interpret such minor incidents as hearing a mouse's squeak or coming upon a weasel.[4] The Arian Constantius, when he wanted to depose the orthodox bishop of Alexandria, had him accused of interpreting signs and making predictions. This was an accusation of impiety only insofar as a Christian should refrain from practicing a reprehensible science. On the other hand, Constantius himself was mindful of omens. Shortly before his death he was terrified by the admittedly disturbing sight of a decapitated corpse that he chanced upon in the outskirts of Tarsus.[5]

Despite the threat of dire punishments, the laws were to remain ineffective. Constantine condemned to the stake those who practiced or led others to practice divination for personal purposes; Constantius introduced a torture probably imported from Sassanian Persia: the "iron comb," which harrowed the sides of the culprit. One can readily see what was targeted: the political dangers of a science capable of indicating, however obscurely, who would succeed a reigning emperor and when. This had nothing to do with persecuting pagans. At the time of the great trials in Scythopolis, in 359, the philosopher Demetrius Cythras did not escape torture; he remained on the rack for some time, but managed to survive by explaining that if he sacrificed it was only so that the divinity would be propitious to him, not to know the future. He invoked custom, that key word of late paganism, and custom saved him.[6]

When pagans represented potential allies, like the pagan clan in the Roman Senate, the emperor was somewhat more conciliatory toward them. During the winter following Constantius' visit to Rome (April 28–May 29, 357), the prefect of the city, Memmius Vitrasius Orfitus, had a commemorative obelisk raised, in accordance with a decision taken when the emperor had been there; this we learn from Ammiamus Marcellinus. But what has been further discovered is the dedicatory inscription of the temple he consecrated to Apollo during the same magistracy.[7] In 359 Tertullus, Orfitus' successor, sacrificed to the Castores (the Dioscuri) so they would calm the sea and a cargo of wheat would thereby reach Ostia; for such a purpose he could invoke Constantine's law of 319 authorizing "white magic."[8]

What is one to conclude about the situation of paganism during the last years of Constantius' reign? That, whatever it was, the emperor had no way of strictly imposing his own legislation on a city when that city's high officials had remained pagan. The outcome depended much more on the power struggle at the local level between Christians and their adversaries.

Two Very Different Bishops

In Alexandria, Bishop George, like Constantius an Arian, had received from the emperor a "long unused" Mithraeum to be transformed into a church. When George undertook to clean and purify the crypt used for initiations, human skulls were found. This detail is probably accurate, though it comes from only one source, the Christian historian Socrates. Socrates, who was writing in the first part of the fifth century, had been the pupil of two pagan philosophers from Alexandria who told him bitterly about the destruction of the cults in their homeland.[9] The top of a skull was indeed found by archaeologists under the cult relief of another Mithraeum, at Königshoffen near Strasbourg.[10] In Alexandria the exposition of those Mithraic skulls immediately caused a scandal. Christians saw them as the remains of divinatory sacrifices; pagans rebelled against the profanation of the sanctuary and started riots in which they gained the upper hand, killing or crucifying many of their adversaries. The transformation of the temple was halted, despite the influential support available to the bishop.

What was involved was not only the local balance of power, but also the individuals concerned. Still under Constantius, in contrast to the activist Gregory of Alexandria, another Arian, Pegasius, bishop of Ilion (ancient Troy), preserved the temples of his city, removing only a few stones for the sake of appearances—and at that from a hostelry attached to one of the temples.[11] Pegasius is a curious figure. When Julian stopped in Ilion at the end of 354—precisely when Constantius was ordering the temples to be closed, though the law may not yet have spread throughout the Empire—Pegasius was delighted to show the young prince the historic monuments of his city, which meant first of all the temples of the gods and the heroes. By then Julian had secretly returned to paganism. Pegasius is not expected to have known that—divulging such a secret could have been fatal for Julian—but did he sense the sympathy of his distinguished visitor for the ancient traditions?

Whatever the case, Pegasius unabashedly justified the fires that burned on the altars and the oil that glowed on the statue of Hector. It was nothing more than the perfectly natural gratitude of descendants of the Trojans toward "a man of stature who had been their fellow citizen." As to the well-preserved statues kept locked within the temple of Athena, in front of them he refrained from making the sign of the cross or any contemptuous hissing. When Julian became emperor and paganism seemed to win out, Pegasius remained "bishop" (*archiereus*), but of the Sun. Was this political opportunism? This unanswerable question is pointless today. What Pegasius' attitude clearly demonstrates is the proximity of beliefs among a number of cultivated minds. Other examples are Heliodorus of Emesa, author of a famous novel, *The Ethiopica*, during the same period, and Synesius at the end of the century.

Julian's reign marks a pervasive reaction. First of all, in the precise meaning of the term, it was a period of restoration: temples damaged by a decade of abandon were repaired, and revenues confiscated by Constantine or Constantius were recovered. In many cases it is because of Julian's actions that we know about the confiscations of temples ordered during the latter part of Constantius' reign, for the benefit or on the initiative of various bishops. That in fact is the primary interest of those actions since the premature death of the young emperor precluded any significant consequences to the recoveries. In Alexandria Bishop George was lynched for having profaned the Mithraeum and because he asked, when passing in front of the temple of the Good Genius (Agathos Daimon, one of the chief patrons of the city), "How much longer will that tomb continue to stand?"

Two officials shared his fate: Dracontius, director of the mint, who threw down an altar that had been installed in the mint building; and a certain Diodorus, in charge of the construction of a church, who ordered that the long curls of little boys be cut so that later the family would be unable to consecrate them at the sacred festival marking the end of childhood. Ammianus Marcellinus, who reports these details, points out that the inertia of non-Arian Christians made it easier for those murders to take place. This is corroborated by Theodoret, a Catholic, who called George "a shepherd more cruel than a wolf, punished by his own sheep." Not only were the victims Arians, and therefore heretics, not only were they supporters of Artemius, the loathed former military commander of Egypt, but in addition, by opposing a local cult and family traditions, they doubtless outraged numerous Christians as well.[12] Constantius himself was convinced that he was protected by his own personal Genius, who ceased appearing to him shortly before he died.[13] Is it not likely that at least some of Alexandria's Christians believed in the Good Genius of their city?

Julian Adrift

Julian kept clear of death sentences. He wanted no martyrs, preferring instead financial harassment. For this reason he decreed that the temple of Asclepius at Aigeai in Cilicia should be repaired at the expense of the bishop who had damaged it. In the way of physical pressure, the most he did was to decide not to punish the Alexandrian assassins of Bishop George; but this was a position that could have caused Christians serious problems had his reign lasted. It heralds the position Ambrose forced on Theodosius twenty years later with regard to the Jews in the affair of the burning of the synagogue of Callinicum. It opened the door to exactions imposed on a community that the laws barely protected any longer. Clerical authors enumerate the profanations and summary executions that seem to have taken place in large numbers in central and southern Syria during Julian's reign.

At times revenge turned into virtual bargaining, as in the case of Marcus, bishop of Arethousa, who held out. He had built a church on a sacred site. The pagans, seeking to have the site returned to them in its former condition, subjected him to dreadful humiliations. His beard was torn out, and he was beaten, dragged through stinking sewers, offered up to schoolboys who jabbed him with their styluses, hung up in a basket, smeared with honey and garum (a kind of brine made of the intestines of fish), all in the heat of a Syrian summer. It came to naught. The pagans could press all the claims they liked, that stalwart character remained intractable. Finally giving up, his enemies let him go and he became a hero for all the Christians in the region, as Libanius ruefully observes, seeing in this a lesson of political moderation.[14]

The emperor did drive Eleusius from his bishopric of Cyzicus for having destroyed temples and converted a number of pagans.[15] But at times he was very awkward in his interventions. In Bostra, Bishop Titus tried to moderate the antipagan fervor of his parish and assured Julian that he was keeping order. The emperor replied in a letter to the people of Bostra: "since he accuses you thus, chase him out of your city on your own initiative." The ploy failed and Titus was protected by his community. The bishop's power stemmed from his popularity in a region where Christianity had been solidly implanted ever since the reign of Philip the Arab (244–249).[16] The Hauran resisted in spite of the milestones that proclaimed at the time not "There is but one God" but "There is but one Julian." This is not to say that Bostra was exclusively Christian from then on; according to Titus, there were just as many pagans.

Different tendencies can appear in fairly close regions, perhaps because our sources are not concerned with the same segments of the population. Apamea, Syria's second city after Antioch (Libanius, *Disc.*, XVIII, 187), was the birthplace of the philosopher Numenius (second half of the second century); at the beginning of the fourth century it had become the seat of a famous school of philosophy, headed by the Neoplatonist Iamblichus, who came from Chalcis on the Belos River, in the same region. Iamblichus had been welcomed to Apamea by a local dignitary, Sopater, who became his pupil and might have succeeded him on his death around 330. Too ambitious for this position, he left for Constantine's court where for a while he was a favorite until he was executed on the charge of being a magician; he was in fact a victim of palace intrigue. As we have seen, he apparently advised the emperor on the traditions to be followed in the founding of Constantinople.[17] His son, Sopater II, remained a celebrity in Apamea until his death in 365.

On a mosaic showing the Seven Sages, found in Apamea, Socrates at the center seems to be teaching the other six who surround him in perfect symmetry. J. and J. C. Balty view this as the pagan transposition of a Christian group depicting Jesus among his disciples, who in this case also number six. The mosaic would seem to have been designed under Julian's personal supervision during his stay in Antioch, late 362 or early 363, and in the name of Socrates would have been intended to glorify the emperor.[18] Such a reconstruction seems a bit fanciful. Anyway, true or not, who better than the Platonists of Apamea could glorify the historical Socrates, master of Plato, and pave his dwelling with such wise maxims as "Use [life] well"?[19] When Eunapius praises Sopater the father, he repeatedly compares him to Socrates for his sagacity and unjust condemnation, and clearly plays on the similarity of their names, which doubtless had been noticed by the Apameans as well. (The Greek form of the name is Sopatros.)

This gentle scene gives no inkling of what was actually

taught by such experts in theurgy as Iamblichus and his disciples. It reminds us that theurgy was only a branch of the much wider learning of those Sages. Sopater had put together a twelve-volume collection of *Various Extracts*, read by Photius who gave him an entry (no. 161, vol. II Henry). It is an anthology of anthologies, an encyclopedia intended for professors and orators; Photius called it a "ready-made general culture" (*polymathian ek tou hetoimou*), of high enough moral caliber to satisfy the demands of his very pious and intelligent reader, the patriarch of the ninth century. The school of Apamea was short-lived. In fact it barely survived Iamblichus, unlike the paganism of the Apameans, who remained faithful to Zeus until the end of the century.

Among other measures instituted by Julian that vexed the Christians were his orders to disinter the Christians buried in Delphi near Castalia, and to demolish a martyrium in Didyma, as well as the tomb of Saint Babylas in Daphne, for reasons of purification: Apollo (divine master of those three places) cannot tolerate the presence of corpses, especially impious ones, near his sanctuaries. But these removals occasionally worked against the emperor. The Christians carried the coffin of Babylas from Daphne to Antioch in a solemn procession, singing psalms.[20] Perhaps Julian was motivated by a passion for classical style: Did the Athenians not cleanse Delos of all its tombs during the Peloponnesian Wars? This is also the attitude of a "puritanical pagan," "obsessed by purificatory rites."[21] And Julian's bad blood led him to simple cunning, complicity with the rioting populace when it was siding with the prince. So Julian congratulates the inhabitants of Emesa, a great center of the Sun cult, for having set fire to Christian churches, which he calls "tombs" with the same contempt expressed by George of Alexandria with regard to the sanctuary of the Good Genius.[22]

In a sense, Julian was also moving toward the creation of a new religion organized on the model of the Christian churches. He reinstituted an office created by Maximinus Daia at the beginning of the century, that of the "high priest" who, for pagans, was equivalent to a bishop for the Christians: the same word, *archiereus*, was used to designate either one. But he went further. In order to encourage a new behavior among his fellow pagans, he bound a duty of charity over these high priests, stating that he was emulating Christian charity: "Don't we see that nothing fostered atheism [that is, Christianity, which denies that there exist several gods] more than kindness with foreigners, attention to burials, false respectability in their way of life? . . . Set up, town after town, a network of homes for guests, so that foreigners enjoy our attention, not only those who share our beliefs, but any of them."

Virtues celebrated in the first part of this letter were not new to pagans. Associations aiming to provide their members with decent burials had always been one of the favorite frames for social life in the Roman Empire. But such virtues were practiced only among members of the same group. Christianity claimed to break down barriers erected by hospitality obligations, membership in burial societies, and similar social conventions. And that is the kind of universalism Julian demanded from his own high priests. But pagan cults were so deeply exclusive that, even had the emperor lived to enjoy a long reign, their devotees would have found it difficult to obey him. Gregory of Nazianzus spoke contemptuously of Julian's "apings" (*pithekon mimemata*), and near the end of the century Ambrose, bishop of Milan, jokes about the useless wealth of temples: "Let them count the captives they delivered, the poor they have been feeding, the assistance they gave to refugees so that they may live!"[23]

This reconstructed religion, imitating ceremonies from the time of the Antonines, failed to convince all pagans. (Julian, following the steps of Trajan and Hadrian, made a pilgrimage to Zeus on the summit of Mount Casios; the last Apis bull in

Egypt was sought and found for him.) It was too austere, too concerned with ritual and not enough with festivals. Julian's taste for sacrifices was not shared by his contemporaries, neither by the intellectuals who tended to make fewer material offerings and, following Porphyry's example, abstained from meat, nor by the people for whom festivals were no longer primarily an occasion to eat meat. Julian's attempt at a pagan restoration suffered from a secularization of butchering.

In Lydia Julian named the philosopher Chrysanthius of Sardis high priest of the province, because auguries warned him against going to the court to serve as the emperor's privy counselor. A native of the region, Chrysanthius proceeded with moderation, "so that in Lydia, one hardly noticed that the cults were being restored" and when the Christians regained power, the province remained peaceful. "He was admired not only because he was capable of foreseeing the future, but because he knew how to put to good use what he had learned." Lydia remained hospitable to pagans until well into the fifth century, in part perhaps thanks to the long and pacifying influence of Chrysanthius, who died at the age of eighty-four. "Long after" the victory of the Christians, perhaps under Theodosius but certainly before the edicts of 391, altars to the gods were restored in Sardis and sacrifices offered by a "vicar of Asia" and a governor of Lydia, both fervent pagans.[24]

Julian's pathetic death at the age of thirty-two—deep within Mesopotamia among the hostile Persians, on the night of June 26, 363, a season and a land in which the Sun he had so ardently worshiped ruled supreme—and the catastrophe that befell the Roman Empire thereafter made him an instant legend. His defenders let it be known that he had been killed by a Christian traitor, an idea that was not displeasing to some Christians. The truth is probably more banal. Julian's death was a *coup de théâtre* that changed nothing. When it occurred, the war was already lost and the fierce reaction that it abruptly halted had failed. But because of it, anyone can re-create the young philosopher-warrior emperor in whatever image he chooses.[25]

Following Julian

The death of the young emperor did not put an end to pagan-ism. Far from it. The decades that followed came under the banner of religious tolerance through an edict published by Valentinian (364–375) at the time of his accession, 26 February 364. Although the edict itself has not survived, we know it from a later reference made by the emperor: "the laws pro-mulgated by me at the beginning of my reign, which allow each individual to observe the religion with which he is im-bued."[26] Actually, during his reign Valentinian avoided inter-fering in the quarrels among Christians. As for pagans, be-ginning in 364 he limited himself to annulling the transfers of property Julian had made to the temples and to prohibiting, on pain of death, night ceremonies.[27] He also undertook mea-sures to separate pagan and Christian religious functions, particularly with respect to civic holidays. Among other rul-ings, no Christian was to be responsible for a temple's keep-ing. After that date the sophisticated ambiguities of a Pega-sius ceased being possible. But, as G. Fowden stresses, those same measures also limited the jurisdiction of bishops over matters directly concerned with public order.[28] In Rome the pagan prefect of the city, Vettius Agorius Praetextatus, re-stored and dedicated anew the portico of the *dii consentes*, the "divine councilors," meaning in this case the twelve Olympi-ans, protectors of the city (367–368).

Valentinian had a younger brother, Valens, whom he ap-pointed coemperor for the East (364–378). Valens, a soldier and "something of a peasant" (*subrusticus*;[29] he had not mas-tered Greek), and an Arian Christian, enjoyed residing in the large and lovely city of Antioch. He also treated it with tolerance—too much so for the taste of the pious Theodoret, Catholic bishop of Kyrrhos, a nearby city: "the slaves of error conducted their pagan mysteries . . . Diasia [festivals of Zeus, patron of Antioch], Dionysia [festivals of Dionysus], and festivals of Demeter were being celebrated once again, not in secret, as might have been expected in a Christian empire, but right in the middle of the agora; that is where the bacchants held their revels."[30]

In spite of these liberal policies, both brothers have been remembered as strict and repressive emperors, particularly in the works of Ammianus Marcellinus and Libanius, both pagans and natives of Antioch. The brothers, for political reasons, were concerned about astrology against which they increased restrictions and instituted a reign of terror. In December 370 they ordered "the activities of astrologers [*mathematici*] to cease . . . public or private, by day or night." They also prohibited the teaching of astrology.[31]

Major trials took place in Antioch in 371–372. An avalanche of denunciations was involuntarily loosed at the time by a high official, perhaps a pagan—the "count of [the emperor's] private affairs" who, along with the "count of sacred gifts," directed imperial finances. This count, Fortunatianus, was hounding two courtiers who owed money to the treasury. They hired a poisoner and an astrologer to rid themselves of this importunate person. But they were denounced. The case, since it involved magic, quickly came before the highest magistrate, the pretorian prefect. The poisoner, arrested and tortured, declared that the plot was a mere bagatelle compared to what else he could reveal: a high official, the former governor Fidustius, had tried to learn the name of Valens' successor.

Fidustius was secretly apprehended and faced with his denouncer. He confessed, with details: he had learned that the successor would be an excellent ruler whose name began with the letters THEOD, but that snoopers would meet with a sorry end. The second part of the oracle was fulfilled at once. As for the first, it was not entirely clear, but Fidustius and his accomplices thought they recognized that "excellent ruler" in Theodorus, second in command of the imperial administration (*secundicerius notarius*). According to the portrait left by Ammianus Marcellinus, he was a charming man, aristocratic and cultivated, not a vulgar peasant like Valens. Not only had they identified Theodorus as the ruler of the augury, but Theodorus had been informed thereof by a vice-pretorian prefect, the "vicar of Asia," who ruled over the provinces to the west and southwest of what we know as Asia Minor: Phrygia, Lydia, Caria, Lycia, and Pamphylia.[32]

The affair went from magic to high treason, and from that to a very dangerous conspiracy, as Ammianus openly acknowledges. The authorities abducted Theodorus, who was in Constantinople, and went about ruthlessly arresting intellectuals and high officials, often one and the same. Once in prison, the rack separated the innocent from the guilty. It also wrested from the perpetrators an account of the consultation—the most detailed document ever found on the practice of magic in the fourth century. Along with the first part of the successor's name, they had managed to obtain the prediction that they would die but would be avenged "on the plain of Mimas" and by Ares, god of war. This is somewhat enigmatic since Mimas is a mountain in Ionia, not a plain.

Ammianus Marcellinus, who reports these details, was convinced of the accuracy of the oracle. Was Theodosius I, Valens' successor, not an excellent ruler? Was Valens not killed in combat on a plain? Granted, it was the plain of Adrianopolis; however, the tomb of a certain general Mimas was observed near the spot where the emperor is assumed to have fallen. If this indication is genuine, it may refer to a local tradition about gigantomachy, well at home in Thrace (I owe this suggestion to F. Vian). In this highly detailed, and assuredly accurate account, the author's beliefs determined the choice

of details and discreetly tinted the overall picture. As Eunapius wisely noted, it is harder to understand oracles than to
procure them.

On the emperor's orders the trials ended in a mass convic-
tion, and Antioch was transformed into a "slaughterhouse."
The carnage was accompanied by pyres of books, "under the
eyes of the judges." Those books were deemed illicit, meaning that they were presumed to contain predictions, or magic
recipes, or astrology. But to appease the perpetrators, the
owners of libraries burned anything at all, treatises on law or
"liberal arts." An experience during the youth of John Chrysostom (he was sixteen or seventeen years old, having been
born probably in February 354) evokes the atmosphere at that
time in the city, surrounded by the army. He was walking
with a friend through the gardens along the river, in the direction of a church outside the city (a martyrium). The friend
saw an object floating on the water:

> He thought it was a piece of cloth, but on coming closer he saw
> it was a book and went down to fish it out. As for myself, I
> claimed my share of the find and joked about it. "Let us see
> what it is first," he said. He opened it and saw magic signs. At
> the same time a soldier came by. My friend put the book in his
> cloak and moved away, petrified with fear. For who would be-
> lieve that we had found that book in the river and pulled it out,
> when everybody was being arrested, even the least suspi-
> cious? We did not dare throw it away for fear of being seen,
> and were equally afraid to tear it up. God finally allowed us to
> get rid of it and we were delivered from the greatest of dan-
> gers.[33]

Books died and philosophers as well. Maximus of Ephesus,
Julian's former councilor, was beheaded. Others were
strangled; some were burned alive, such as the philosopher
Simonides, whose fate Ammianus compares to that of Pere-
grinus, a Cynic philosopher, who in 165 set fire to himself at
Olympia. Was Simonides a martyr of paganism? Surely not.

Of philosophy? Perhaps. In Ammianus' eyes he was first of all a victim of tyranny and an example of the freedom and constancy that true wisdom bestows.[34] While this witch-hunt was going on in Antioch and Asia Minor, Libanius kept a low profile. He undertook to burn the copies of his letters, beginning with those written in the summer of 365, when a pagan, a cousin of the late Emperor Julian, had attempted to seize power.[35] That is why his collected correspondence, so precious to us today, includes so few letters between 365 and 388 (he died in 393). Libanius had yet two close calls: one during the trial of a patron of athletes when he might have been compromised; the other when a friend who would not have withstood torture was about to be arrested (it was Libanius' good luck that the friend suddenly died before his arrest).[36]

Despite all this, on May 29, 372 the emperors authorized official soothsaying in the Roman Senate and "all religious customs allowed by the ancestors" (*omnis concessa a maioribus religio*). "We do not condemn [soothsaying] but prohibit its use for harmful purposes."[37] It is in this legal context that the official sacrifice mentioned earlier could be performed at Sardis.

• • •

ON his death in 375 Valentinian left two sons, Gratian, then sixteen, who was living in Treves, and Valentinian II who was four. When their uncle Valens was killed by the Goths at the battle of Adrianopolis on August 9, 378, Gratian appointed as Augustus for the East, Theodosius, a Spanish general who restored order after the defeat (January 19, 379). Policy toward pagans does not seem to have been affected by this. On June 17, 379, Theodosius renewed permission for the magistrate who directed the Olympic games in Antioch (the *alytarchus*) to cut a cypress in the sacred woods of Daphne and to plant others there, in the name of "custom," that custom which pagans unceasingly claimed as their right.[38]

The reason for such tolerance is not hard to see. At the beginning of his reign, the first concern of Theodosius, a confirmed Catholic, was to contend with heretics (Arians). The most he did, on May 2, 381, was to deny apostates the right to draw up wills, an indirect attack indicating that changes of religion do not all go in one direction.[39] He did, however, continue to treat eminent pagans with favor. When Vettius Agorius Praetextatus died in 384, he was at the peak of his career, pretorian prefect for the West and consul designate. The epitaph his wife composed for him recalls the merits he acquired during his years of service, not only to the Emperor but also to the old gods. That same year in Constantinople, a "court pagan," Themistius, was prefect of the city. In the East a law of 381 renewed the prohibition against going to the temples to learn the future, by day or night, and authorized "pure prayers" but not "maleficent incantations."[40] As Libanius later confirms, Theodosius permitted hymns accompanied by offerings of incense and prohibited live sacrifices associated with magic. He went no further than Constantine and Constantius, and expressed himself far less truculently than the latter.[41]

Prudence and moderation are also evident in a law of November 30, 382, which exceptionally allows the governor of Osrhoene (the region of Edessa) to keep open a temple in which the ceremony of New Year greetings (*vota publica*) took place, so long as no sacrifices were made and no oracle was consulted. Thus the people could see the statues, "which must be appreciated for their artistic value rather than for their divinity."[42] The authorization to look at cult statues with admiration smacks of euphemism. Ten years later the laws that will prohibit any manner of pagan cult specify that "one must not raise one's eyes to the statues," evidently because that is tantamount to an act of adoration. It is not even known which temple was referred to. Since Edessa was partially at least a Christian city from the beginning of the third century, it was supposed that the temple was in some other city of Osrhoene, such as Batnai, which had remained pagan. This is a pointless supposition since we are sure that pagans remained in Edessa until the end of the sixth century, and the ceremony of New Year greetings assuredly took place in the capital of the province. It is evident from other sources that a margin of freedom was granted to traditional celebrations. Cult statues were dedicated in a Mithraeum, a private sanctuary, at Sidon in 389.[43]

The most curious example is surely that of Ephesus. It proves to what degree the language of mythology had survived even in circles that were officially and wholeheartedly Christian. A catastrophe, either a fire or an earthquake, had destroyed the district west of the street of the Kouretes. Major reconstruction was therefore begun toward the end of the fourth century. A wealthy lady of the city, a Christian named Scholastikia, undertook at her own expense the repairs of the baths, and to this end used the columns of a building that must have collapsed during the same catastrophe, reducing it to a quarry. It happened to be the sanctuary of Hestia "of the Council" (Boulaia), preeminent civic deity and patron goddess of the sacred hearth of the city.

At the same time, the highest provincial authority, the proconsul of Asia and also a Christian, had undertaken to restore the temple near the baths that was dedicated to the Emperor Hadrian. This meticulous restoration even added an embellishment: a recycled frieze older than the temple, depicting the legend of the city's founding, was placed inside the building and finished with a plaque that showed on the left, the assembly of the gods around Selene, the Moon, identified with Artemis; and on the right, the deceased father of Theodosius, Theodosius himself, his wife, and their son Arcadius, grouped around Artemis who appears thus a second time as the patron deity of Ephesus. In front of the temple the proconsul dedicated a statue of Theodosius' father (a Spanish general of the same name, executed at Carthage in 375). It is possible to date these restorations with precision: after 383, when Arcadius was named Augustus, which accounts for his presence on the frieze, and before 387, when the proconsul of Asia, Nummius Aemilianus Dexter, was appointed to other offices.[44]

The discrepancy between Scholastikia's project and the governor's is not as great as it might seem. What the restoration of the temple expresses above all is respect for the traditions of Ephesus and veneration of the imperial family. These sentiments took the established forms of the dynastic cult, just as they did fifty years earlier, at Hispellum in Umbria. Although Christians, the emperors accepted this cult devoted to their person, which was never confused with that of the traditional gods.[45] The association of the Olympian gods with Theodosius father and son, and the preeminence of Artemis among them, only served to enhance the universal power of the emperor and consecrate his legitimacy (the elder Theodosius, it would seem, was a *novus homo*), and to glorify the city of Ephesus.

In point of fact, from the beginning of Julian's reign (361) until after the first measures taken in the West by Gratian under the influence of Saint Ambrose (382), pagans enjoyed freedom of worship which Constantius' laws had interrupted for only a few years. Paradoxically, though the emperors were Christian, apart from Julian who died June 26, 363, and the usurper Procopius in the East (September 28, 365, to May 27, 366), the traditional religion continued to enjoy state subsidies and to regulate the calendar with its festivals. In this light, the suddenness of the upheavals that occurred during the decade of 390 is all the more stunning.

· 56 ·

· 5 ·

Toward the Interdict

BY 382 the court of Gratian, son and successor of Valentinian, had moved to Milan from Trier. Gratian, then twenty-three, fell under the influence of Ambrose, bishop of Milan. Ambrose, who had previously served as governor of northern Italy, now succeeded as mentor the poet Ausonius, the young emperor's preceptor in Trier, who was a very moderate Christian in political matters. Ambrose was much more dynamic, and undoubtedly he was responsible for convincing Gratian, toward the end of 382, to reenact Constantius' ruling of 357 and once again to remove the altar of Victory from the Senate. Gratian surpassed his predecessor by eliminating the pensions paid by the imperial treasury to pagan priests, and by refusing to fill vacant positions in the sacerdotal colleges. When a deputation of senators came to ask him to rescind those measures and to remind him that officially he was the chief of the State cults—probably around the beginning of 383—he refused to receive them and with great ostentation dropped the title of *pontifex maximus*. These gestures marked a "separation between paganism and the State."[1]

By that time the commander of the armies in Britain, Magnus Maximus, had probably already rebelled and the pagans could say: "If Gratian does not want to be *pontifex*, Maximus will soon be *pontifex*" (or, "there will be soon a *pontifex maximus*," the phrase being equally ambiguous in Latin and in Greek).[2] Gratian was assassinated on August 25, 383, at the instigation of Maximus, whose attempt at usurpation was partly successful: from 384 to 387 he was recognized by Theodosius, who was reigning in the East, as Augustus for Gaul and Spain, and residing in Trier. Gratian's younger half-brother, Valentinian II (he was only thirteen in 384), kept the remainder of the West and resided in Milan where he rejected a second request from the Roman nobility to replace the altar of Victory in the assembly room of the Senate.

These repeated attempts should not lead one to believe that the Senate was a homogeneous pagan assembly. In 382 Pope Damasus organized a counterpetition on the part of Christian senators, and in 384 Ambrose declared that there were more Christians than pagans in the Curia.[3] Nonetheless, the pagans still set the tone. One of their most conspicuous representatives, Q. Aurelius Symmachus, who was prefect of the city, drafted on this occasion an official "report" (*relatio*) that has remained famous. Like Libanius' speech *For the Temples*, written about the same time or in 389–390, it was a plea for paganism, "the religion of our fathers," warrant of Rome's political greatness and also one of the many paths to the divine. "What does it matter by which wisdom each of us arrives at truth? It is not possible that only one road leads to so sublime a mystery."[4] But what power could tradition, clear insight into the interests of the State, and an all-too-human wisdom have against Revelation?

As for Maximus, the hopes the pagan party had risked on him were disappointed, although Symmachus sang the praises of the usurper, having composed a panegyric to him. Maximus was in fact a fervent Christian, given moreover to confiscating the property of senators, as they were also great landowners. He tried to eliminate Valentinian II, invaded Italy, and was defeated and killed at Aquilea (August 28, 388), not by the weak Valentinian but by Theodosius, who readily forgave Symmachus.

At that time, from 384 to 388, the only secure power in the Empire was in the hands of Theodosius. He chose as pretorian prefect for the East one of his Spanish compatriots, a man of trust and a very committed Christian, Cynegius. Theodosius reminded him that sacrifices to examine the liver and entrails for purposes of divination were prohibited.[5] In these instructions Theodosius was merely recapitulating the laws of Valentinian I, and he did not go further when he forbade Cynegius to name a Christian as high priest in Egypt (the title merely designated the imperial administrator of temples and pagan priests).[6] Cynegius interpreted these measures as very restrictive toward pagans, and in 384, during a tour of inspection in Egypt, he closed the temples and forbade all sacrifices, thereby provoking, as Libanius complained, "useless agitation."[7]

An Uproar over Temples

It was probably Cynegius who in 386 provided Marcellus, bishop of Syrian Apamea, with the troops needed to carry out the demolition of the great temple of Zeus in that city of "Apamea, which continued to honor Zeus whereas elsewhere people were punished for honoring the gods."[8] According to Theodoret, writing before 450, this was the first time the destruction of a sanctuary was prompted by a bishop who had official, if not imperial, support, because of the large number of pagans in the region.[9] Theodoret has left a vivid description of the event: the prefect arrives with his troops and tells the Apameans to remain calm; the soldiers try in vain to knock down the temple; the Apameans are afraid of the army, but the army is probably afraid of what is inside the temple.

Then intervenes an ordinary laborer, who digs a mine under three columns of the peristyle. But the fire in the trench will not start, so they have to awaken the bishop from his midday nap. He sprinkles the trench with holy water—"one would have thought it was oil"; and when the three columns fall, carrying with them twelve others and the wall of the temple on the same side, a terrible roar rouses the city from its summer drowsiness and attracts a stunned crowd to the ruin, too amazed to do anything but stare in silence. It takes little effort to imagine the hatred aroused by the bishop, and the disillusionment of the devotees of Zeus, seeing that their god's only defense was to take the form of a blackish demon that momentarily prevented the fire from lighting—Zeus, reduced to a few puffs of smoke from unseasoned wood!

Marcellus wanted to begin the systematic destruction of all the temples, "thinking that this was the easiest way to convert" the population. He was killed shortly after, while attempting to destroy a temple at Aulon, in the district of Apamea. He was captured and burned alive during the assault, which had been launched with "soldiers and gladiators"; this time (389?) he evidently had a private militia at his disposal. His children demanded to avenge their father, but the regional assembly stopped them, arguing that "he had been deemed worthy of dying for God." This reply smacks of a polite refusal. The assembly had no desire to disturb the public peace any further.[10]

Probably around 388–390—by which time the East was administered by a pagan, Tatianus, pretorian prefect—Libanius published his plea *For the Temples*, in which he traces a picture of the religious climate of the time. Theodosius upheld the interdiction against immolating victims. But he left the temples open, and did not prohibit fire, incense, or fumigations. He continued to allow freedom of conscience and to treat pagans favorably. This often moving account reveals all of Libanius' apprehensions, particularly concerning the Serapeum in Alexandria, whose beauty and usefulness he praises repeatedly in this plea. The cult celebrated there assures, he says, the flooding of the Nile and thus the prosperity of Egypt and the Empire. The danger comes from below, from the unscrupulous monks and bishops who supported Cynegius. Libanius describes their gangs scouring the countryside, sacking and destroying temples, assaulting and robbing peasants suspected of making sacrifices.[11] His position is intentionally that of a responsible administrator and politician; the advantages to be gained from the temples, not all of them magical, had to be weighed in the balance.

As Libanius tells it, Cynegius, encouraged by his wife, thus demolished a temple-citadel, strategically placed near the Sassanian border, with strong walls and a terraced roof from which one could sight deep into enemy territory, and as large as the city it protected. Given the date, one might expect Libanius to be deploring the destruction of the temple of Zeus in Apamea, but Apamea is not a border city, and the description is better suited to a building of Semitic type. If Libanius made no mention of what happened in Apamea, it is probably because the destruction was more or less official. The temple he describes contained statues of iron kept in darkness, "shunning the light of the sun"; it has not been identified with certainty. Ever since the seventeenth century, scholars have proposed two sites, Edessa and Carrhae. Edessa has been eliminated because none of its temples was as large as the city; moreover it had the reputation of being impregnable because of its citadel.[12] The temple of the Moon God Sin at Carrhae would make a better candidate.[13] It did indeed stand on the hill of the citadel, and Carrhae's fortifications were not good. Libanius, in his funeral oration for Julian, describes it as the "vast and ancient sanctuary of Zeus"—a purist like him would never speak in Greek of a masculine Moon God.[14]

Another important sanctuary of the region also comes to mind, that of Hierapolis, accurately described in the second century by Lucian, a native of the area.[15] Its temple of the Syrian goddess was reputed to be one of the great works of Semiramis (the one described by Libanius was "without equal"). It was built on a hill and surrounded by high walls that formed a double enclosure. Libanius' mention of "iron statues hidden in the darkness, shunning the light of the sun" would refer to a scene described by Lucian: the raising of the statue of "bearded Apollo" (Nabu). The statue was carried on a litter by the priests, but before they entered the doors of the temple it was attracted upward—by a magnet placed in the ceiling, as has been since long understood. One more fact in favor of Hierapolis should be added: cult practice seems to have vanished there in the course of the fourth century, to judge from Julian (in 363) and Egeria (in the spring of 384).[16] Hierapolis, though on the western bank of the Euphrates, was an important strategic place in the struggle between Rome and the Sassanians. So it would have been true that the main significance of the temple, at the time of Libanius' plea, was military, as was the case for many others, large enough to be used as barracks, well-built enough to be used as strongholds. Libanius could vindicate its ruin without speaking on behalf of a place of forbidden worship. In fact he does not even name the patrons of the temple. On the contrary, the cult of Sin in the city of Carrhae continued well into the Islamic period.[17]

Perhaps it was to quiet the unrest caused by Cynegius' zealotry that a pagan was appointed prefect for the East after him: Tatianus (388–392). Cynegius, however, remained in favor, for in 388 Theodosius chose him as his colleague in the consulate for the following year. He was not at all repudiated for having upheld, with the authority of a high official, the persecutions led by certain bishops. (There are no accounts of the destruction of temples during that period in Greece, which was outside the control of the prefect for the East.) Religious questions were not crucial to the careers of Theodosius' collaborators; he indulged State notables, local officials, and civil servants and took little interest in the clashes between Syrian peasants and the monks who were beating Christianity into them. He did intervene when order was threatened in a large city: an edict for Egypt, dated September 2, 390, orders the monks to return to the desert—in other words, to quit Alexandria.[18]

Between Fire and Massacre

At first, Theodosius' position toward pagans had been cautious. From 388 to 391 he remained in the West with Valentinian II. After that, the supreme authority which they incarnated together initiated measures that treated pagan cults rudely. Why the reversal? Was it the influence of the redoubtable Ambrose, a far more difficult partner for the emperor than the bishops in the East? Ambrose, who had first been a high official, had the stature and the knowledge of a statesman, and as early as the end of 388 he demonstrated it. At that time he prevented Theodosius from securing reparation for the Jews of Callinicum, on the Euphrates, after a band of fanatics—once again, monks instigated by the bishop—had burned their synagogue and a sanctuary attributed to some gnostics, the Valentinians. Based on the report of the count (military governor) of the East, the emperor, generally protective of the Jews, had at first ordered the bishop to rebuild the synagogue. Ambrose pointed out that in the eyes of the people, one of the causes of Maximus' fall was his punishing of the Christian arsonists who burned a synagogue in Rome. Theodosius did not insist.[19]

For the next two years Theodosius, displeased by this intervention, kept the bishop of Milan at a distance and grew closer to the Roman aristocracy. In 389 a friend of Ausonius from Bordeaux, the rhetor Latinius Pacatus Drepanius, delivered to the Roman Senate a panegyric of the emperor that contained no reference to Christianity. Theodosius was hailed as a god, *deus*, which in truth was hardly compromising, as we have seen in connection with the reliefs from Ephesus.[20] He appointed pagans—Aurelius Victor the historian (389), and later Ceionius Rufius Albinus (from June 17, 389, to February 24, 391)—as prefects of the city and also as consuls in Rome for the year 391 (Fl. Tatianus and Q. Aurelius Symmachus). This benevolence toward individuals was not reversed, even after the attempt to restore paganism in 392–394, and it earned him their gratitude. In 404 Claudian, court poet but a pagan nonetheless, described him as "the best of deceased princes," *optimus ille/divorum*, using for "deceased" the consecrated term *divus*, meaning "deified."[21]

A dramatic episode brought the bishop of Milan back to the forefront. As a result of a law of March 390 condemning homosexuality, the commander of the troops in Illyricum, residing in Thessalonica, imprisoned a charioteer who was very popular in the city and who had made advances to the general's cup-bearer. Was he really protecting threatened virtue, or assuring for himself exclusive rights to a tender youth? That is not clear, but it did arouse tension between the population and the commander, Boutherichus, who was moreover a German. On the eve of important races the city, exasperated by the arrest of a star contestant and by the billeting of foreign troops, revolted. Boutherichus was killed by the rioters.

In reprisal, Theodosius ordered a massacre, accounts of which vary slightly from historian to historian. According to Rufinus, the population was assembled in the circus under the pretext of a spectacle and encircled by troops who killed indiscriminately. According to Sozomen, Theodosius set the number of victims, who were then rounded up by the soldiers; they even arrested travelers arriving in the city. A father begged one of the patrols to take him in place of his two sons, offering a sizable bribe. The soldiers rejected the deal, for it would have left them below their quota. In this account, the population was decimated like a mutinous regiment: 7,000 dead.[22] Rufinus' version, written from Aquilea in northern Italy a few years after Theodosius died, is more generous toward the emperor, holding the German troops responsible for the enormity of the massacre. Sozomen, on the other hand, may be suspected of a rhetorical device. Loving his two sons equally, the father is unable to choose which one he will save, and saves neither (like Buridan's ass, which was both hungry and thirsty and died of exhaustion at equal distance from a bucket of water and a feedbag). The first part of this dreadful anecdote is illustrated in literature by other examples, from the *La Clemenza di Tito* to William Styron's *Sophie's Choice;* in which the Nazis replace Theodosius' henchmen.

In Milan, Ambrose required that Theodosius expiate this crime and denied him communion until he had made an act of penitence. He was readmitted to communion in time for Christmas 390. The emperor's antipagan measures can thus be explained as a consequence of his repentance. But beyond the immediate circumstances, they mark a new and definitive course of action in Theodosius' religious politics. During the decade of the 380s Theodosius, a Catholic who succeeded Arian princes, was primarily concerned with heretics, for whom he established the principle of constraint in matters of faith, and apostates who had left Christianity. In 391 it was the turn of the pagans, after an initial offense in 389 when he turned their holidays into workdays.[23]

The Fall of the Serapeum

On February 24, 391, an edict published in Milan and addressed to the prefect of the city of Rome prohibited all blood sacrifices. This was tantamount to a general interdiction of pagan cults: "No one is to go to the sanctuaries, walk through the temples, or raise his eyes to statues created by the labor of man." A similar edict, dated June 16, 391, issuing from Aquilea, was addressed to the prefect and to the count (military governor) of Egypt regarding Alexandria. It was immediately used by Theophilus, the bishop of that city, to destroy the main temple, the Serapeum, and other sanctuaries in and around the city.[24]

Theophilus first obtained authority over an abandoned building—a temple according to some, a basilica according to others—in order to make a new church out of it, and he mockingly displayed the sacred pagan objects he had found inside. This caused an uprising, and the Serapeum was turned into a fortress commanded by the Neoplatonist Olympius. Theophilus' role in Alexandria was that of a provocateur, as G. Fowden rightly says.[25] Contrary to Marcellus of Apamea, he kept a low profile during the police operations that followed the riots and that led to the siege of the Serapeum.

Olympius, discouraged, secretly fled before the sanctuary fell to the soldiers, after explaining to his followers that the statues had lost their power, the divine *dynamis*, which had gone back to the heavens. He reached Italy and was not heard from again. Two other valiant defenders of Serapis, Helladius and Ammonius, emigrated to Constantinople. They taught literature and served the priesthood, one of Zeus, the other of Thoth-Hermes. Only the first activity was still overt; in their classes in Constantinople they brooded over the indignities inflicted on the baboon Thoth by the "infidels," and Helladius boasted that he had killed, in hand-to-hand combat, nine of the attackers.[26] It was seemingly during the exodus of pagan intellectuals after the fall of the Serapeum that the poet Claudian left for Rome, where he found himself Christian protectors, the Anicii, and where he had a brilliant career.[27] Another poet and professor of Greek, Palladas, remained in Alexandria even though his stipend from the city had been canceled. He wrote of his despondency:

The defuncts once left the lively city;
And we who continue to live bring the city to burial.[28]

Not only did the gods not react to their humiliations, they seemed to rally to the side of their victors. When the Serapeum was demolished, interior walls covered with hieroglyphs were exposed to sunlight. According to experts consulted at the time, certain signs in the form of a cross signified "future life" (which is correct: this is the sign *ankh*). It supplied a seasonable symbol: the gods of paganism vanished at the appearance of the cross of life hidden in their bosom. Sozomen seems to have taken this quite literally; Socrates, more rational, sees a mere coincidence.[29] As for the statue of the god, it was the work of Bryaxis, a famous Athenian sculptor of the fourth century B.C. It belongs to the category known as "chryselephantine": works put together on a wooden armature of diverse materials, in particular gold and ivory. Its beauty, opulence, and the amazing skill that went into using the techniques of goldsmithy for a statue of large dimensions all contributed to its prestige. It was broken into pieces by the Christians, who razed the marvelous edifice, symbol of the city, and the most important monument in the Empire after the Capitol in Rome, according to Ammianus, who was writing before its destruction.[30]

In the next period a text that could have been considered a commentary on the catastrophe seems to have enjoyed some popularity, to judge from the fact that, having been at some time translated into colloquial Latin, the form in which it has come down to us, it is quoted by Saint Augustine in *The City of God* (written after 410). It is a prophecy allegedly placed under the patronage of Thoth-Hermes, god of mystic wisdom. The treatise in which it appears, titled *The Perfect Discourse*, was probably written in Egypt in the second or third century. Its roots lie in a very old tradition of native Egyptian apocalyptic literature, foreseeing a culmination of evil upon earth just before the ultimate triumph of Justice. Here Hermes is speaking about Egypt, "image of heaven," and "temple of the entire world."

A time will come when it will seem that the Egyptians, in the piety of their hearts, have honored their gods in vain with a devoted cult . . . The gods, on leaving the earth, will return to heaven; they will abandon Egypt . . . That holy earth, land of sanctuaries and temples, will be completely covered with coffins and corpses. Oh Egypt, Egypt, nothing will remain of your cults but fables, and later, your children will not even believe them! . . . For the divinity will return to the sky; the people, abandoned, will all die, and then with neither gods nor men, Egypt will be nothing but a desert. It is to you I speak, holy river, it is to you I announce the things to come: torrents of blood will swell your waters to their banks . . . and there will be more dead than living; as for those who survive, it is only by their language that they will be recognized as Egyptian: in their manners they will seem to be men of another race.

Saint Augustine interprets this text as "the wild cry of the demons who foresee the punishments that await them" (VIII, 23 f.); medieval theologians also made use of it.[31] How could it be read after the event of 391 in Alexandria? Some scholars supposed it had been altered then in order to "foretell" that last collapse, but it has been proved to have stood in its Greek form at the time of Lactantius, that is, at the beginning of the fourth century, prior to any antipagan edict.[32] Though concerned in fact with the demise of native Egyptian ("pharaonic") cults, it might have offered some bitter comfort to the defenders of the Serapeum. But first of all it was precious to their adversaries. It appeared to them as one more proof, administered from inside, that the old faith was definitely doomed to death.

Contrary to the expectations of such pessimistic pagans as Libanius, in the summer of 392 the god of the Nile inundated the Egyptian countryside as always and fertilized it with his silt, mindless of the sacrileges committed the year before. He did not send torrents of blood or create a hecatomb among the people. The presence of that glimmering ribbon of water must have caused more confusion than we can imagine among all those who, like Libanius, believed the prosperity of the Empire depended on the accomplishment of the ancient rites. The rising of the Nile was certainly a familiar event, but also, nonetheless, admirable and amazing every time it occurred, one of the prodigies of nature in which pagans of Late Antiquity saw a divine presence. Once more heaven blessed the impious.

The fall of the Serapeum was a more spectacular event than the pious vandalism that broke out at the same time around Alexandria, or even the destruction of the temple-citadel of Hierapolis (or Carrhae). The anxieties that emerge from Libanius' *For the Temples* lead one to believe that the attack on the Serapeum had been planned in advance. It seems likely that Ammianus, when comparing it to the Capitol, emblem of Rome's eternity, and emphasizing the importance of its library, deliberately presents it as a building of political and cultural rather than religious significance. As in Aigeai, Apamea, and later Gaza and Carthage, the fervor elicited by a pagan sanctuary only embittered the hostility of the bishop and quickened its ruin, through a process that meant something quite different from the recuperation of an out-of-use basilica to be transformed into a church. In the impetus of the taking of the Serapeum, other temples were pillaged and destroyed, in Alexandria and in Canopus.[33] Paganism in Alexandria had been dealt a very hard blow.

The Edict of 392

The fatal blow to the ancient cults was not delivered until new political problems had arisen in the West. Valentinian II was a puppet in the hands of his army commander, Arbogast, a confirmed pagan of Frankish origin (which did not keep him from boasting about his closeness with Ambrose). When Valentinian decided to get rid of his burdensome commander-in-chief, Arbogast, in the emperor's presence, tore up the letter of dismissal he had received. Shortly thereafter, on May 15, 392, Valentinian committed suicide, or was strangled by order of Arbogast, who then placed on the throne a professor of rhetoric, Eugenius. The new emperor, a nobody it would seem, was a Christian, who had a philosopher's beard, which made a great impression after all the clean-shaven military men in that office. From 392 to Theodosius' victory of September 4, 394, Rome went through a period of feverish soothsaying and pagan revival. The animating spirit of all this was Virius Nicomachus Flavianus—a Roman aristocrat from a great family allied with that of the Symmachi. Flavianus became Eugenius' pretorian prefect. The altar of Victory was restored to its former place as was the financing of the traditional ceremonies.

The decisive battle between the troops of the usurper and those of Theodosius, who had returned from Constantinople, was fought near the river Frigidus, in the region of Aquilea. It seemed to symbolize the confrontation of the two religions: the Cross on the pennants of the Christians against Hercules on those of the pagans, who had set up statues of Jupiter on the surrounding hills to stop Theodosius. But an ill wind blinded the pagans whom their gods failed to protect. They were crushed, Eugenius was executed, and Arbogast committed suicide, as did Virius Nicomachus Flavianus. As the civil war was about to begin, he had received an oracular assurance of victory.[34] He could not endure defeat or the loss of his illusions. A fiasco of such proportions smacked of divine judgment.

During the course of the next generation the Roman aristocracy rapidly converted to Christianity. It had held out until then for political reasons, because the grandeur of Rome (and the prosperity of its patricians) seemed linked to respect for tradition. After the battle at the Frigidus it was no longer possible to believe this. Psychological factors entered into the collapse of Roman paganism. The "judgments of God," which came into fashion then, were generally unfavorable to it. Luck, the old *felicitas* of the Romans, was now on the side of the Christians.

It was during Eugenius' usurpation that Theodosius totally abolished all freedom to practice pagan cults with the notorious law of November 8, 392, addressed to the new pretonian prefect for the East, Flavius Rufinus who, unlike his predecessor, Tatianus, was a pious Christian: "No one, under any circumstances, is permitted to sacrifice an innocent victim nor, as a less serious sacrilege, to worship one's lares with fire, one's genius with uncut wine, one's penates with perfume, to light lamps, waft incense, or hang garlands." The punishment was death for the maker of blood sacrifices, a fine and confiscation of the place of the crime in the case of a domestic cult: "offering incense to a divinity, decorating a tree with ribbons, or raising an altar with bunches of torn-up grass."[35]

The historian Zosimus relates an address in which Theodosius, after the victory over Eugenius in the autumn of 394, announced to the Senate that from then on the treasury would no longer pay the costs of the cult or the sacred sacrifices of the Roman religion. Whether or not this is accurate, the decision to rescind Eugenius' restorations was bound to take place. After Gratian's financial restrictions of 383 and those of Theodosius in late 394, it was Theodosius' sons who in 396 published an edict addressed to the pretorian prefect for the East that revoked the privileges accorded to pagan priests, "ministers, prefects, hierophants, or whatever the title that designates them."[36] On the political level, Theodosius treated the usurper's partisans with indulgence.[37]

Freedom of conscience was not definitely suppressed; it would not be until 529, under Justinian. It is worth notice that solemn public ceremonies, celebrated by pagan priests, were not themselves abolished. Once sacrifices and prayers were prohibited, what remained? Processions, entertainments, and spectacles whose disappearance would have met with too much public outcry. Nearly a century earlier, even the extremely austere bishops at the Council of Elvira had been unable to deny them to their adherents. There seems to have been a considerable discrepancy between the desires of the subjects in many regions and various social classes and the instructions of the laws. It was no small thing to withdraw all State support from pagan ceremonies. Some disappeared. The ancient games in the Greek style, Olympic and others, were very popular under the High Empire, especially in the second and third centuries. Many cities, such as Antioch, prided themselves on their festivals organized on the model of the Olympic, Pythian, or Actian games.[38] Those festivals whose ritual still retained a religious character were abolished shortly after 392. Despite some local reluctance, the decrees of prohibition only hastened the shift of public taste, which preferred "hunts" or animal fights to athletic or musical contests.

· 6 ·

After the Defeat

THE decade from about 392 to 402 saw an outpouring of laws, some of which have been preserved in the Theodosian Code. Some of them complete and define each other; others correct and in some cases seem to contradict each other. This is because they refer to local situations of which, for the most part, we have no knowledge.

Time of Troubles

The events in Carthage beginning in 399 are one of the rare exceptions. That year the two counts Jovius and Gaudentius made a tour of Africa, "demolishing temples of the gods and breaking their statues," supported by the crowd.[1] But there were still many pagans: "How great was the power of the goddess Caelestis in Carthage!" Saint Augustine later exclaimed. And the devotees of that goddess, who is none other than the very ancient Phoenician 'Anat, Punic Tanit, deeply resented the profanations, even though her vast temple had been merely closed and not demolished.

This doubtless explains the tone of the law addressed to the proconsul of Africa in August 399 by Arcadius and Honorius, sons of Theodosius, who died in 395: "Just as we previously abolished profane rites by a salutary law, so we do not permit the abolition of gatherings of citizens for holidays, or the gaiety everyone shares." The holidays will be allowed "when the people wish it," as long as they are not accompanied by sacrifices or any "unlawful superstition." At the same time the emperors inform the proconsul of Africa not to try to demolish the temples, so long as they do not contain anything illicit (*illicitis rebus vacuas*).[2] These conciliatory provisions did not restore complete order. On June 16, 401, Saint Augustine exulted, telling how Christians in Carthage, shouting "Rome and Carthage are the same!" have shaved the golden beard off a statue of Hercules. During the decade of 410 agitation in Africa continued. At Sufes in Byzacene (today Sbiba, 100 kilometers west of Kairouan in Tunisia), after Christians had destroyed another statue of Hercules, the main god of that city, the riots that ensued resulted in the death of sixty Christians. In 408, at Calama (today Guelma in Algeria), pagan dancers attracted a crowd, Christians were roughed up, and church buildings were set on fire.[3]

In Carthage the temple of Caelestis, after having been closed for a number of years, was turned into a church for Easter. An eyewitness, Quodvultdeus, who later became bishop of Carthage, left a vivid account of the event. The temple had been condemned for some time, its approaches littered with garbage and overgrown with brambles. The pagans claimed it was watched over by snakes and vipers. A throng of Christians, led by Bishop Aurelius, entered and consecrated it to the One God. The bishop immediately seated himself on the empty throne (*cathedra*) of the deposed goddess and announced the transformation of the building into a "cathedral" church. However, a prediction circulated among the pagans that the temple and the avenue that led up to it would be restored to the ancient cult; they were, in any case, remaining sacred. So in 421 the authorities decided to have the temple razed to the ground. But it took a catastrophe such as the fall of Carthage to the Vandals in 439 to plunge the site of Tanit's temple and its avenue into the oblivion in which it still remains.[4]

The law of 399 concerning holidays applied only to a particular region and cannot be regarded as pertinent elsewhere. During the same period, other measures, whose political context is known to us, can be compared or contrasted with them. The festival of Maiouma, authorized in 396, was prohibited on October 2, 399, for reasons not of "superstition" but of immorality.[5] It nonetheless endured at least until the eighth century and at times was celebrated in a completely official way. Also in 399, although the proconsul of Africa was receiving the orders just described, the prefect of the Spains and the "vicar of the five provinces" (roughly speaking, the south of Gaul, what today is Aquitaine, Languedoc, and Provence) were advised that "at the same time as we prohibit sacrifices, we want the decorations of public buildings (*publicorum operum ornamenta*) to be preserved"—it was not a matter of tearing to pieces any old statue.[6]

In the East, however, the situation described by Libanius some ten years earlier in his plea *For the Temples* had remained unchanged. On November 1, 397, a law addressed to the count of the East ordered that the stones of destroyed temples be used for public works, such as the repair of roads, bridges, aqueducts, and fortifications. This would seem to suggest not only an intention to scatter the stones and profane them, but surely also the magnitude of the destructions.[7] At the beginning of the fifth century (in 405), John Chrysostom, native of Antioch, bishop of Constantinople, and formerly Libanius' auditor, encouraged from his exile in Armenia the gangs of monks who pillaged the sanctuaries in the Phoenician Hills. When the peasants of Phoenicia massacred or wounded the overzealous missionaries, Chrysostom urged those who re-

mained uninjured to hold on, "like pilots in a storm or doctors when fever rises." He also provided them with more material aid, seeing to it that they had enough clothing, shoes,
and food, and giving them money for overseers and work-
men to demolish the temples.[8] In spite of this, whereas the
Amanus Mountains north of Antioch became studded with
churches, Mount Lebanon resisted. This makes it easier to
understand how in Damascus in 399, the pretorian prefect
was instructed that the demolition of temples in the countryside should proceed "without mobs or riots" (*sine turba ac tumultu*).[9] The central authority, administered by the young emperor of the Orient, Arcadius (born in 377), tried to control
uprisings it had not started and to maintain civil order as well
as it could.

At the other side of the Empire, this was the period when
Martin, bishop of Tours (ca. 371–397) began his missions to
christianize the Gallic countryside. As in Syria, the monks in
Gaul played an important, though less brutal, role. It would
be unfair not to compare this image of "God's raiders," which
we shall find again in connection with Hypatia and which is
also reflected in the invectives of Libanius and Eunapius
against the "men in black," who "eat like elephants," with the
portrait of the ascetic, seen from within, precisely by John
Chrysostom: "They train to live like the angels; neither the
men nor the women marry, they barely sleep and eschew all
comfort; with the exception of a few, they have even become
incorporeal."[10] These were not necessarily other people; they
could be the same ones in other circumstances.

Gaza, a Pagan City

Among the major changes during that period when the appearance of very important cities like Alexandria and Carthage was suddenly altered, none is better known than the
demolition of the temple of Zeus Marnas at Gaza (May 402),

directed by Bishop Porphyrius. Thanks to Marcus the Deacon's biography of him, we can see with unequaled precision the reactions of the common pagan people.[11] Porphyrius was the first bishop to refrain from overstepping the law in his operations against the temples.[12] He was contending with a formidable rival: a totally pagan city whose temples had remained active, although its port, Maiouma, had been Christian since the time of Constantine. At the outset of his bishopric (January 2, 396), Porphyrius was unable to gather more than 280 believers. To reach his diocese he had to travel a road that the peasants had strewn with brambles, thorny twigs, and garbage, and on which they burned smoky, foul-smelling substances that stung the eyes of the bishop and his retinue. The entrance into Gaza took place at nine in the evening, in darkness (on the 20th or 21st of March 395).[13]

This arrival was the exact opposite of the solemn entrance (*adventus*) of a bishop or a magistrate. In such cases the roads were smoothed, the streets swept and scattered with flowers, the people waved palm fronds (whereas on the road to Gaza they threw palm thorns, *scolopes*, before the bishop's train), and incense was burned before the officials. Here the "foul-smelling substances" must have been cowpats, a common fuel in the region, with a pungent smell and stinging smoke. In a society so concerned with ceremonial, what a jibe! Marcus the Deacon sought to arouse the reader's indignation at the treatment meted out to the bishop. Even allowing for the rhetoric in this parody of an *adventus*, one can imagine the anguish that must have seized this little convoy as it hurried through hostile villages at nightfall.

Not until 398 did Porphyrius succeed in having the temples of Gaza closed, and, even so, the Marneion continued to be used in secret. But the bishop wanted more; he wanted the temple of Marnas destroyed. Violence of that kind posed a grave political problem, and the emperor, Arcadius, was aware of it when, probably in October 400, he replied to the bishop of Gaza: "Well do I know that your city is full of idols. But it is prompt in paying taxes and contributes much to the treasury. If we were suddenly to terrorize these people, they might flee and we would lose considerable revenues." [14] In order to achieve his goals, the bishop ingratiated himself with the empress, who was then pregnant, by predicting that she would give birth to a son, which she did shortly thereafter. It still took a good bit of maneuvering and the occasion of the little prince's baptism for Porphyrius finally to obtain, early in 402, a decree from the emperor to demolish the temples in Gaza—eight in all, to be destroyed by imperial troops between the 12th and 24th of May of that year. The prospect of pillage encouraged the fervor of the soldiers. [15]

During this period the ancient cults seem to have been crushed. The bishops attacked the most vigorous and revered sanctuaries—that of Zeus in Apamea, of Serapis in Alexandria, of Marnas in Gaza. Fortunately for the pagans, not all the dioceses had bishops like Porphyrius, energetic, clever, and lucky enough to force the hand of the master of the world and secure military intervention. It is nonetheless clear that the time of humiliation had arrived for them, with all the violent reactions in its wake. The marble facing of those parts of the Marneion that were prohibited to women was used to pave the square in front of the temple, so that not only women but animals as well sullied it constantly! For years afterward the women of Gaza continued to avoid stepping on those stones. [16] A few years after the destruction of the temple there were riots over a question of property, leaving the pagans masters of the city for at least two days. [17]

A Problem Resolved

During the first part of the fifth century, many laws concerning pagans still remained, even though the emperors spoke as though the problem had been resolved: "the pagans who remain, although we believe there no longer are any," said Honorius and Theodosius in 423.[18] In keeping with a policy whose spectacular applications we have already seen, those laws aimed first of all at discouraging believers by profaning their sanctuaries. To the legislator's eyes, paganism was a religion of place. To refute a god, he seized the place where that god was said to reign. What was to be done with the great plethora of abandoned buildings? This problem was an old story in cities where paganism was in the process of being stamped out. In Constantinople, as of 386 the temple of Aphrodite had become a garage for the chariots of the pretorian prefect. The temples were no longer kept up after a law of 408 confiscated their revenues and turned them over to the army. "Orders were often given" to demolish altars and pull down statues. Temples in imperial domains were to serve other uses, and individuals were obliged to destroy their own altars and statues.[19] As a rule the emperors protected their patrimony and recycled it. They destroyed only the old private sanctuaries, because it was more difficult to determine whether they were still being used for pagan cults.

While sacrifices and prayers were prohibited, legislation was more flexible or more hesitant about festivals and processions. At the beginning of the fifth century the "Athenian people" voted to raise a statue to a sophist, Plutarchus, who had three times subsidized Athena's processional boat in the great festival of the Panathenaic games.[20] This was an entirely official honor. It must have occurred before the law that confiscated temple property, for that law also prohibited banquets and "any kind of pagan celebration" and empowered the bishops "to prevent these practices." (It was the only one that confirmed the role of the bishops.) That same law also affected a form of social (and familial) life that was very popular in all of Antiquity. It was logical for the two measures to be linked: the revenues of the temples also made it possible to organize their festivals.

The festivals died hard. In 434–435, Leontius, prefect of Constantinople, sought to reestablish the Olympic games in Chalcedon, on the eastern bank of Bosporus, just opposite the capital. After failing because of the forceful intervention of a certain Hypatius, abbot of a nearby monastery, he then, pretending to be sick, recrossed the strait to the capital. Leontius' attempt had encountered no opposition from the bishop of Chalcedon. It was only after the fact that the bishop, filled with contempt for Hypatius, ordered a scholar to draft a memoir on the pagan character of the Olympic games, which originally had not struck him. As for the prefect, he was neither impious nor a provocateur. In later years he founded a sanctuary in Thessalonica to Saint Demetrius, still the chief protector of that city. Not everyone drew the boundary between religion and entertainment along the same lines.[21]

An edict of 435 finally ordered the destruction of the temples, "if there are any still untouched."[22] It was directed against those buildings that had not already been profaned, to the exclusion of those that had been reused or at least emptied of their religious contents, as was doubtless the fate of the major monuments in large cities. Not only were there some remaining after fifty years of increasingly more efficient demolitions, but at the end of the sixth century the "inquisitors" were still able to round up a number. As is always the case, the simplest cults were the hardest to eradicate. During the first part of the fifth century (between 400 and 446), Hypatius and his monks descended on the rural sanctuaries of Bithynia to cut down the sacred trees. This, it would seem, was entirely on his own initiative.

It is not surprising that paganism persisted so close to the capital, in the province where three hundred years earlier Pliny the Younger had been concerned with the large number of Christians. The wooded hills along the Black Sea are very hard to penetrate, even today, and that is the region where Hypatius vented his missionary zeal. The open countryside outside of Nicomedia and Nicea and the plain of the Hypius River, along with the cities of the Pontic coast, may have gone over to Christ, but the inhabitants of the isolated valley of the Rhebas, though much closer to the capital, kept their ancestral festivals.[23] Many centuries later a similar contrast would be seen in Thessaly, between the islamicized plain and the villages of Mount Pelion that remained Christian. Hypatius followed the example that his spiritual father Jonas had given him in Thrace, where one finds the same kind of topography. But how could he hope to cut down all the sacred trees in the Bithynian forests (called today the Sea of Trees, *ağaç denizi*)? This mad woodcutter's enterprise could not possibly succeed, and the tree cult has survived to this day, in that province as in others.

The Fall of Rome

The most resounding event of the early fifth century, one that left all the subjects of the Empire bewildered whatever may have been their religious beliefs, is incontestably the catastrophe of August 24, 410. Alaric captured Rome and let his army sack it for three days. This was not his first incursion through the Roman Empire. In 396 he had already "visited" Greece. On that occasion the pagan historian Zosimus praised the efficacy of a cult dedicated to Achilles, established in Athens since the reign of Valens. Athena and Achilles appeared to the Visigoth king, and he called off his attack on the city; so says Zosimus (V, 6). The reality of the event was probably less miraculous. In the West the Vandal general Stilico, who served in the same capacity as guardian of the young emperor Honorius (eleven years old at the death of his father in 395) as had Arbogast to Valentinian II, defeated Alaric in 401, and another Gothic chief in 405, and negotiated with Alaric between 406 and 408.

Stilico was relentless in his hostility to pagan cults. It is to him that Saint Augustine attributes the authorship of the laws for Africa in 399.[24] One day in Rome his wife Serena removed from the statue of the Great Mother a beautiful necklace, placing it around her own neck. Stilico himself had the gold scraped from the doors of the temple of Jupiter on the Capitoline, probably early in 408, to pay a ransom to Alaric.[25] One of his enemies accused him of having burned the Sibylline Books, kept on the Capitoline, which contained prophecies for the whole of Roman history. This is surprising, for Christians were not fundamentally hostile to the Sibylline Books, which they counted among the precursory texts of their own faith; in much later times, the Sibyls even found a place among the frescoes of the Sistine Chapel, alongside the prophets of the Old Testament. Shortly before the sack of 410, Saint Melanie on leaving Rome predicted its fall, referring to the Sibyl and couching her language in Sibylline terms. If Stilico was hostile to the Sibylline Books, it was likely as a statesman, that is, for their apocalyptic and very defeatist views rather than for strictly religious reasons. It may have been the same concerns that made him leave the statue of Victory in the Curia (the statue, not the altar, which had been taken down some fifteen or twenty years before).[26] In any case, the pagans did not base their judgment of him on such measures. Eunapius, like most contemporary authors, attacked him violently, whereas Olympiodorus praised him. His greatest panegyrist was a pagan, Claudian.[27]

In 408 Honorius, fearing Stilico's ambition, had him, his family, and a number of his followers arrested and executed. Alaric took advantage of this to lay siege to Rome where famine was then raging, but he withdrew in exchange for a ransom. He returned in 409 and forced the Senate to accept a usurper, the incumbent prefect of the city of Rome, Attalus, a pagan from Asia Minor, who had been given a most noble name of that country, the dynastic name of Pergamum's Attalids more than six centuries earlier. Attalus gave Alaric the satisfaction of naming him "commander in chief of the two armies" (infantry and cavalry; *magister utriusque militiae*), a post he had long coveted. From that time on he followed the Visigoths, first in the king's train and then in that of his successor, Athaulfus. In 410, finding Attalus less docile than he had expected and being unable to negotiate with Honorius who had fled to Ravenna, Alaric turned against Rome and pillaged it. He died of an illness shortly afterward, in Cosentia in Bruttium (today Cosenza in Calabria). The romantic narrative of his funeral is well known: he was buried by his men with treasure from Rome in the bed of a river whose course had been diverted and then restored.

As Zosimus presents it, contrasted with the rescue of Athens by its divine protectors, the sack of Rome in 410 could be seen as a punishment sent by the neglected gods. Saint Augustine wrote *The City of God* to propose a better explanation. The pagans' argument had simplicity in its favor: at last the gods were reacting, they who had not kept the Nile from rising after the destruction of the Serapeum. Celestial justice came with its usual delay. While Alaric was laying siege to the city, the Etruscans suggested that the prefect undertake conjuring ceremonies that earlier had saved the city of Narni. Strongly tempted, the prefect nevertheless consulted the pope who set the condition that the ceremonies remain secret, which put an end to negotiations. Such ceremonies could only be efficacious if they were official, accomplished at the expense of the State, with the participation of the Senate. If the anecdote is true, it would be wiser not to draw any conclusions about the solidity of the pope's religious beliefs. In such emergency cases, it is his intransigence that should be noticed. And even if the anecdote were invented by the pagans, it remains very revealing: the pagan religion could be suitably practiced only within the framework of the State, municipal or imperial.[28] As for the prefect, Gabinius Barbarus Pompeianus, he was massacred by the mob, not because he was a pagan but because of a riot over wheat in the midst of a dreadful famine. In 410, on the other hand, another official, quite overtly pagan, Tertullus, was extremely popular.[29]

Attalus, the puppet set up by Alaric, had himself baptized as an Arian, adopting the faith of his Visigothic masters who used him again in 414–415. His acts and his gestures are of little importance, nor are those of his consul Tertullus, who addressed the Senate as "consul and pontifex, offices of which I hold the first and hope to obtain the second" (Orosius, VII, 42, 8). During those troubled times both factions— that of the legitimate emperor Honorius as well as that of Attalus—felt that any kind of help was worth seeking, and the pagans hoped to gain some advantage thereby. It would seem that in July–August 409 Honorius gave verbal instructions (an *oraculum*) of tolerance to the count of Africa in order to encourage the loyalty primarily of the Donatists, who were heretical Christians. This tolerance was revoked on August 25, 410.[30] After the sack of Rome various pagan colleges were authorized to return to Rome. Those concerned were people engaged in spectacles: "companion-dancers of Cybele"; bearers of flags, insignia (some in the shape of snakes, *dracones*), or statues; fortune-tellers, storytellers, and the like.[31] These emergency measures were rescinded as soon as the situation returned to normal. In 415 a law for Africa required that pagan priests return to their native cities, which meant that they were expelled from Carthage and were in a manner of speaking under house arrest. The holdings of their associations were confiscated.[32]

The Western Empire underwent a brutal collapse, during the course of which the great cities disappeared. Mention of the fate of a few representative examples hardly gives an adequate picture of the situation; suffice it to say that with the cities a culture was destroyed. Trier was devastated by the Vandals, the Suebi, and the Alani, who crossed the Rhine on December 31, 406, wandered through Gaul, and remained in

Aquitaine until the autumn of 409 before descending first into Spain, then, a generation or so later, about 429, passing over into Africa. They took Carthage in 439. After the Vandals, the Visigoths—who came from southern Italy where they had buried their king, Alaric—settled for a time in Aquitaine. When they left for Spain in 414, they sacked and burned Bordeaux. The hardships caused by these invasions led to episodic revivals of paganism in various places.[33]

Hypatia

For the most part those were grim years for all. For the pagans, they brought only illusory improvements. The moving figure of Hypatia has been used repeatedly as a symbol of their crushing defeat. Daughter of Theon, a famous Alexandrian mathematician who taught her mathematics and astronomy, Hypatia was beautiful and intelligent. Author of commentaries on older writers, she also studied philosophy and gave lectures on the different schools. Her disciple Synesius, a great landowner from Cyrene who became bishop of Ptolemais in Cyrenaica and continued to write to her even after his ordination, communicates the enthusiasm she aroused. Her coterie should not be mistaken for a hotbed of pagan agitators, nor, even less, of magical or astrological practices. Had this been the case, Synesius could not have borne witness to her teaching with such effusion. She was given a post subsidized by the city, and seems to have taught a kind of high-level vulgarization of philosophy to an audience of pagans and Christians who rubbed shoulders without any difficulty. Hypatia discussed "all kinds of schools," but she was above all committed to a very traditional kind of Platonism, little influenced by Plotinus or Porphyry.[34]

An unconfirmed anecdote, which places her in a provocative light, suggests that she shared the opinion of the ascetic Christians of her time, considering the body "a pile of garbage."[35] She showed her menstrual pad to a member of her audience who had fallen in love with her, saying: "That, young man, is what you have fallen in love with, and there is nothing beautiful about it." She seems to have been as devoted to her virginity as a Christian nun. This story has been thought to have been made up by a biographer, attributing to Hypatia the behavior of the cynical philosophers who "acted like dogs," meaning that they mocked all shame, like the noble Hipparchia who, eight hundred years earlier, had sex in public with her husband, Crates. But the cynic model surely influenced Hypatia herself, not merely her biographer, for she wore a short tunic [*tribon*] "and was not ashamed to mingle with men."[36] The manners of the cynics had been fairly well accepted by Christians of Late Antiquity; moreover, the lives of the saints provide numerous episodes that in our eyes are equally shocking. There is no reason to deny the authenticity of this one merely because of taste. Though chaste, Hypatia was not disembodied.[37]

· · ·

PREFECTS sent by the central power hastened to meet her on their arrival. Her influence was felt particularly by the one in charge in Alexandria in 415—Orestes, naturally a Christian—when she was assassinated. Not only was Orestes powerless to protect his mentor, but the conflict that arose between him and the bishop, Cyril, was directly responsible for Hypatia's death. In contrast with Orestes, Cyril was a native of Alexandria, the nephew of Bishop Theophilus who had ruined the Serapeum. Orestes had become exasperated by the bishop's constant intrusion and surveillance. Their antagonism was recounted in three episodes and with great understanding by the Christian historian Socrates, a contemporary.

The first episode, set amid the bustling life of a great town, with its factions, riots, and night dangers, began in the theater. In Alexandria, as elsewhere in the Empire, people were very fond of pantomines, a kind of silent mimetic dance, performed by a main interpreter, accompanied by an orchestra and sometimes a choir, on themes analogous to those of classical theater. The audience acclaimed favorite dancers, taking sides and often excitedly even coming to blows. Theater, as long as it existed in the Roman and then the Byzantine empire—that is, well into the sixth century—led to violent rioting.[38] It served to crystallize factional hatred; in Alexandria, in 412, this was confessional, Jews against Christians. Thus, on Saturday, a day of rest for the Jews, scuffling became commonplace. The prefect sought to restore some order and sat in the theater (which was not unusual) to take the necessary steps—in short, a kind of police exercise. Bishop Cyril there sent his followers, led by a schoolteacher, Hierax, who acted also as the head of a claque for the bishop's sermons. The Jews charged Hierax with provoking disturbances; the prefect saw him as a spy of the bishop, and had Hierax arrested and tortured publicly. The infuriated bishop then convened the heads of the Jewish community and threatened them (with what, Socrates does not say) if they did not keep the peace.

The situation deteriorated. The Jews, having agreed on an identifying sign (a ring made of palm fibers), arranged nighttime sallies to beat up Christians. They might also have decided to burn, again by night, the church known as Alexander's church. But the rumor spread, Christians ran for help, and Jews allegedly murdered every person they encountered who was not wearing a ring of palm fibers. This at least is the version told by Bishop Cyril in order to justify the ensuing reprisals he led, as he destroyed synagogues and expelled Jews from the city, confiscating their property. The event impressed his contemporaries for, Socrates reminds us with no little gravity, Jews had lived in Alexandria ever since its foundation. Orestes, whose authority was challenged, took this matter greatly to heart and informed the emperor. In vain, it would seem, and from then on hostility reigned between the bishop and the prefect.

In the second episode Cyril tried to gain the upper hand. With the help of a cohort of five hundred monks brought from the desert monasteries south of the city (Nitrun), he fomented a revolt against Orestes. When the prefect's chariot passed through the streets, the monks gathered crowds and accused him of being a "sacrificer" and a pagan ("Hellene"). Orestes, at first on the defensive, justified himself, declaring that he was already baptized (many Christians at that time were baptized late in life, after they considered themselves worthy of the sacrament). A particularly excited monk threw a stone at the prefect, hitting him in the head and causing blood to cover his face. That was too much. The fanatic was arrested and tortured to death by the prefectorial police. Once again the prefect and the bishop informed the emperor, while the body of the monk was exposed in a church as a martyr for the faith. Cyril gave him a new name, that of a saint. This recalls a pagan usage by which the dead were often heroized, becoming the object of a funerary cult, under another name. But the moderate Christians of Alexandria did not support their bishop, feeling that the victim had only paid for his crime, so the advantage this time was the prefect's.

Unable to attack his adversary directly, Cyril—and this is the third episode—avenged himself on a figure from his entourage. Some time after the attempt on the prefect's life— during Lent, when fasting and religious exaltation encouraged violence, as it did many times in the future—Hypatia was returning from a trip when fanatics dragged her from her carriage into one of the town's main churches, which was the see of the patriarch. This church, though it had been dedicated to Saint Michael, was still known by the name of the pagan sanctuary whose walls it reused: the Caesareum (center of the former imperial cult in Alexandria).[39] There Hypatia was stripped, stabbed with shards of pots and crocks, then hacked to pieces. The remains of her body were paraded around the streets of the town and finally burned—a repulsive custom that was neither a Christian innovation nor peculiar to Alexandria.

Explanations of this explosion of hatred vary. According to the pagan Damascius, who wrote at the beginning of the sixth century, the bishop, passing Hypatia's house and seeing the crowd gathered there, discovered how popular this philosopher was. This version places direct blame on the bishop and makes the murder a clear expression of the hostility between Christianity and pagan philosophy. But it is most unlikely that Cyril, who was made bishop in October 412, would not have learned about Hypatia's celebrity before March 415, since it had been already established for ten if not twenty years.[40] It was not a child prodigy or a young girl who was tortured in 415, but a mature lady. Her legend began with Damascius and continued until Hugo Pratt sketched her silhouette in a night scene in Venice—heiress of Alexandria and Byzantium, permeated with occultism.[41]

According to Socrates, who here is a much more reliable historian than Damascius, the bishop considered Hypatia an obstacle to his reconciliation with the prefect. She would have been the victim of her own political influence (as a native of Alexandria, she could provide useful advice to an administrator who was a stranger to the city) and of the struggle of two factions. To Orestes' resources of police, arrest, and torture, Cyril replied with riots. While we cannot determine the bishop's exact responsibility in this tragic story, his hands cannot have been entirely clean, since the murder was committed in his own patriarchal church. As in so many other cases of rioting, the guilty went unpunished, even though the name of at least one of the leaders was known. Such cruelty was criticized, even by fervent Christians. Marcus the Deacon as well as the author of the Georgian *Life of Porphyry* tell us about a controversy between a Manichaean "Elected" woman (Marcus), or a pagan priestess (Georgian translation from the Syriac) and the pious bishop of Gaza, which is ended by an act of God that resulted in the sudden death of the girl, and by the funeral that the bishop allows her corpse—the whole intended to enhance the superiority of Saint Porphyry of Gaza over his contemporary, Saint Cyril of Alexandria.[42] But Hypatia was not killed for reasons of militant paganism. The fact that she was a pagan simply made her more vulnerable in a conflict that concerned the municipal life of Alexandria.[43]

· 7 ·

Political Exclusion

 $\mathbf{P}$ AGANS increasingly were kept out of power. An edict of November 14, 408, for the first time prohibited enemies of the Christian religion from serving the palace, which was to prove "far more decisive than rulings against the cults."[1] From then on, it was dangerous for a high official to be a pagan or to be considered one. But this edict was immediately rescinded through the forceful intervention of the barbarian chief Generid, count (military governor) of Italy at the time the law was promulgated, and subsequently of Illyricum, able defender of the Empire and devoted to "ancestral traditions" and cults of the gods. A victorious general could take such liberties, as we have seen in the case of the Frankish general Arbogast. In Constantinople in 400, the Gothic chief Fravitta, after ridding the emperor of his compatriot Gainas, had no qualms about professing his fidelity "to the ancestral gods and customs," even within the emperor's hearing.[2]

On December 7, 416, pagans were excluded from the army, the administration, and the judiciary.[3] In 423 Honorius and Theodosius II reinvoked the old measures taken against them. Two months later they lightened the punishments provided for those caught making sacrifices (confiscation of goods and exile instead of death), and accorded their protection to pagans who "cause no trouble."[4] This law also applied to Manichaeans, Montanists, and Jews. The pagan problem had lost its specificity. The law's new clemency can be explained by the well-known reluctance of Theodosius II to order executions.[5] But pagans had not yet disappeared, and the death sentence would be restored three times during the years that followed: in 435; on January 31, 438, during a time of famine "caused by the cults of demons"; and on November 4, 451, after the death of Theodosius II, in the case of the proprietor of a place where the cult was practiced.[6]

What was the result of those measures, and in particular the exclusion of pagans from the administration after having served in large numbers throughout the fourth century?[7] A. Lippold, echoing an opinion of modern historiography that even under Theodosius II pagans were still close to the throne, regards that emperor as having treated the holders of "the ancient beliefs" with "magnanimity" because his wife, the poetess Eudocia, was the daughter of a pagan rhetor.[8] Alan Cameron has vigorously contested this argument. Although Eudocia, daughter of the rhetor Leontius, was born a pagan and originally named Athenais, she was converted before she was married. There is no reason to believe that her conversion was mere lip service, nor that her genuine Christian faith interfered with her taste for classical culture.[9]

Throughout the century, barbarian generals continued in the political forefront both in the East and in the West. They were, however, no longer pagan but Christian—either Arian, as in the case of Aspar of the Alani (a tribe of Iranian origin), or Orthodox, as in the case of Tarasis of the Isaurians (a barbarian people from the interior of Asia Minor). Aspar was powerful in Constantinople for forty years under three emperors (431–471). Under Theodosius II (January 10, 402–July 28, 450) he defeated a usurper in Italy (424–425) and the Vandals in Africa (431–432), though he was later defeated by Attila with whom he negotiated or fought from 441 to 449. Theodosius' sister and counselor Pulcheria chose as her brother's heir to the throne Marcianus, a subaltern of Aspar; when Emperor Marcianus died in 457, Aspar imposed his own candidate, Leo, who reigned from 457 to 474. But after 466 Aspar's influence was eclipsed by that of another general, Tarasis, son of Codisas, who called himself Zeno. In 471 Aspar was assassinated, along with his son Ardabur, by imperial order; this gained the emperor Leo the nickname of "butcher." While on occasion these individuals may have shown favor to one pagan or another, this no longer implies that they supported paganism.

Cyrus of Panopolis, a very high official during the reign of Theodosius II and also a distinguished poet, was thought to be a pagan. Prefect of the City and of the Praetorian Guard for the East in 439–441, consul in 441, he fell suddenly from grace in August 441, or very shortly thereafter, because his popularity irritated the emperor. He also fell victim to the intrigues of the eunuch Chrysaphius, the emperor's chamberlain. Cyrus was in effect charged with practicing paganism. Cameron, however, has demonstrated that this notable, who while in power founded a famous church of Virgin Theotokos, was certainly a confirmed Christian by the time of his magistracies.[10] Later exiled to Cotiaeion in Phrygia as a bishop, he gave a sermon of unimpeachable orthodoxy, as erudite as it was concise, on the Christmas following his dismissal: "My brethren, let us honor in silence the birth of God, Jesus Christ our Lord, for the Word of God was conceived in the Virgin Mary through hearing alone. Glory to Him forever and ever. Amen."

Cyrus was quite simply a cultivated Christian, imbued with classical culture. Because he was a native of Panopolis, in Egypt, where paganism had remained influential in intellectual circles, he was particularly vulnerable to such a charge.

Cameron compares the situation to the McCarthy era in the United States: loose accusations—since the Christian population of Constantinople did not really understand what the charge meant—impossible to refute (if the behavior of the accused was exemplary, it was the better to hide his beliefs), and dangerous, all the more because the death penalty for practicing paganism had been restored in 435 and confirmed again in 438.

Aside from Cyrus, there is an example of a declared pagan who held official functions under the same regime. This was Olympiodorus of Thebes, who was also a poet and a historian of the period 407–425. A great traveler, he was a member of an embassy sent to the Huns in 412.[11] There he was involved with a certain Donatus, who was deceived by a false oath and assassinated, apparently by the ambassadors who subsequently offered gifts from the emperor to the supreme chief of the Huns to appease his anger. The entire story is known only through Photius' résumé of Olympiodorus' own account: "He speaks of Donatus, of the Huns, and of the great skill of their leaders as archers; the historian himself went among them as an emissary to Donatus. He relates the dramatic tale of his agitated and perilous voyage by sea, and recounts how they deceived Donatus with an oath in order to kill him, in defiance of all laws, and how Charaton, the first among kings, became furious over this murder but, thanks to imperial generosity, he calmed down and made no trouble." This brief text leaves many questions unanswered.[12] Who was Donatus? A Hun chief? Or a turncoat, which would better explain how representatives from Rome dared murder him?

This uncommon ambassador also went into the Great Oasis (Khargeh) in 421, and among the Blemyes in southern Egypt, the latter on the invitation of the "chiefs and interpreters of the gods" of the pagan Blemyes who were interested in him because of his reputation.[13] The Blemyes are doubtless those unnamed barbarians who, according to Olympiodorus' admirer the philosopher Hierocles, bestowed great honors on him. But meaningful honors at the Roman imperial court, or even a role of any importance, they certainly were not. For in his mission to the Huns, Olympiodorus appears to have played the part of a secret agent. His career seems entirely representative of the way pagans were pushed aside under the reign of the cultivated but pious Theodosius II. At the same time, the insistence with which Hierocles evokes the pagan priesthood of the Blemyes unquestionably reveals something about Olympiodorus' curiosity: in those lands he could see a religion that was directly descended from pharaonic Egypt being practiced out in the open, one whose tradition had not been lost. Classical paganism, which had been a state religion that regarded its priests as magistrates of a sort, could not survive in secrecy without changing fundamentally. Olympiodorus' interest, under its ethnographic facade in the manner of Herodotus (he borrowed the term *historia*, "investigation," to designate his travels), was linked to his faith.

• • •

PAGANS continued to serve in the hierarchy of the Eastern provinces, however. Aspar, at the height of his power, came into conflict with a magistrate, perhaps a governor, named Severianus, a native of Damascus and a committed pagan. Severianus wound up losing his post but not his faith. Later, Zeno offered him the pretorian prefecture if he converted, but Severianus refused. A glance at the personality and career of this scion of an excellent family is warranted. We know about him solely because of Damascius, his fellow citizen.

Severianus, who had been destined by his father for the lucrative career of lawyer, must have done some studying at Beirut. But he was more interested in poetry and philosophy, and the premature death of his father allowed the young man to pursue his interests under the tutelage of Proclus in Athens. His assertive character later made him an admired, and original, literary critic. Did he not despise the poet Callimachus, that model of elegance, to the point of frequently "spitting on his book"?

In court Severianus, an upright judge, was quick with his death sentences, and he himself attributed his downfall to the excessive harshness of his opinions. And finally, in politics arrogance led him to attack those who were much more powerful than he—Aspar, and one of his sons, Ardabur. A dream he had depicted his vehement and ultimately impotent character. Severianus saw himself as a driver—which could have meant that he would play a political role—but instead of a chariot, he was driving a mountain; however powerful he might think he was, he would get nowhere, for no driver could move a mountain. As his biographer Damascius succinctly says, "the executive side of him had the upper hand over the deliberative."[14] One would have to be an eccentric like him to choose his philosophical and religious notions over the pretorian prefecture.

Severianus remained important enough to become implicated in a plot against Zeno with one of Aspar's surviving sons. Denounced by his accomplices, he managed to get off, though we do not know how. That same Severianus who was destined to fail was counted by Damascius among those who tried to defend the cause of paganism. A middling hero for a lost cause.

The Rebellion of Illous and Pamprepius

The most intense hopes for the restoration of paganism in the fifth century were probably those that accompanied the rebellion of Illous in 482–484, in which the pagan poet-astrologer Pamprepius played a determining role. Not that there was any thought of placing a pagan emperor on the throne. Illous was a Christian who rigorously observed the decisions of the Council of Chalcedon (451). There is no clue that he would have retained his astrologer had he been victorious, still less that Pamprepius' counsel would have led him to condone outward exhibitions of paganism.

Illous' revolt must be seen in the context of the attempts of the Isaurians to secure supreme power; its religious aspects are secondary. Isauria was a mountainous region bordering the southern coast of Asia Minor, which had survived in virtual independence since the third century. From time to time its inhabitants came down to pillage the territories of the interior or coastal cities; the emperors, unable to follow them into the Taurus glens, surrounded their lands with military colonies and fortified outposts. At the beginning of the fifth century the Isaurians extended their incursions well beyond Anatolia, all the way to Phoenicia and Galilee. In the northeast they posed a threat to the city of Armenia where John Chrysostom was exiled. But their leaders, like those of the tribes pressing against the gates of the Empire, were only too delighted to place their forces in the service of the central power for their joint profit.[15]

The first Isaurian to obtain a post as a high staff officer was no less than a "commander in chief of both armies" (*magister utriusque militiae*) by the name of Zeno, at the end of the reign of Theodosius II (447–451). At the time of his death Zeno, according to ancient evidence (Damascius), was rumored to have been planning to assassinate the emperor.[16] The second Isaurian, also a general, was Tarasis, son of Codisas, who took the name of Zeno, which sounded better than Tarasis, in memory of his compatriot. He married the daughter of the emperor Leo and, as we have seen, helped him eliminate Aspar and his clan in 471. (Aspar had tried to kill Zeno two years before; in 471 Zeno saved the life of Aspar's youngest son and gave him his granddaughter in marriage.) At the age of seven, Zeno's son was proclaimed emperor by his grandfather Leo in 471 and succeeded him as Leo II that same year. Three weeks after his coronation, small Leo II crowned his father coemperor; ten months later he died from an illness. From that time on Zeno reigned alone until his death in 491, except for a brief moment, 475–476, when a brother-in-law of Leo I usurped the throne. Zeno inaugurated a new power and, during the troubles that occurred in the early years of his reign, thanks to Illous, the pagans were close to the throne for the last time.[17]

Illous, supported by the excellent troops that the tribes of the Taurus provided, was the third Isaurian to gain power. Though a close friend of emperor Zeno, he nonetheless took the side of the usurper against him in 475. But when the usurper did not keep his promises, Illous had a change of heart and restored Zeno to the throne in 476. It is not surprising that in 477 one of Zeno's slaves tried to assassinate him, as did a factotum of the queen mother in 478, and agents of the empress in 481. Nor is it surprising that Illous rebelled in 484, especially since his victories were making him very popular. He released the queen mother from prison where he had been holding her since 478, and in Tarsus made her proclaim another Isaurian, Leontius, emperor in July 484. In September, Leontius and Illous were roundly beaten near Antioch by Zeno's army and sought refuge in Isauria in a fortress where the queen mother soon died. The usurpers managed to hold out for four years against imperial forces; when the citadel finally fell in 488 it was because they had been betrayed. Three years later Zeno died without an heir. His wife, the daughter of Leo I, gave the crown to Anastasius, an esteemed palace official (a "silentiary"), rather than to Zeno's incompetent brother. In the Taurus the Isaurians revolted, but in the end they were defeated (497), their leaders executed, and themselves deported to Thrace.[18]

Ambition, not religion, dominates this entire episode, which was a struggle of clans within an ethnic group, and of individuals within the imperial family. Religion, in the eyes of the modern reader, is lacking in these conspiracies and battles. At best it was a pretext, since Illous and his family claimed strict fidelity to the Council of Chalcedon, whereas Zeno and Anastasius sought a compromise with those whom the council had condemned—the Monophysites who held the majority in Syria and in Egypt. Questions of dogma were not at stake. Once their rebellion was crushed, the Isaurian deportees had no difficulty serving Anastasius. And anyway, this religious quarrel concerned only Christians.

The pagans of the time were primarily interested in a person close to Illous, his adviser and astrologer, the shrewd Pamprepius. Many hopes were born then.

> "Remember," said a veteran of this adventure who afterwards became a Christian, "how many sacrifices we offered in Caria, as pagans to the gods of the pagans, when we asked them, those supposed gods, while dissecting livers which we examined by means of magic, to tell us whether with Leontius, Illus and Pamprepius and all those who rebelled with them, we would conquer emperor Zeno, who died a pious death. We received a multitude of oracles and promises as well that emperor Zeno could not withstand their revolt, that the time had come for Christianity to dissolve and disappear, and that the cult of the pagans would return. However the events proved that the oracles were lying, as happened with the oracles given by Apollo to Croesus the Lydian and to Pyrrhus the Epirote."[19]

This declaration by a disillusioned partisan of Illous indicates how his revolt looked to the pagans: like the battle of the Frigidus in Italy nearly a century before, once again God seemed to be handing down a judgment on the two religions. In the end, the worth of a religion is measured against its practical efficacy. Pamprepius soon paid for the errors of his astrological calculations. He was decapitated within the Isaurian camp, his head tossed out to the besiegers. As for those who feverishly dissected the livers of their sacrificial victims, they sadly converted to the stronger religion.

Not all of them certainly. This same declaration offers elements of a pagan reply to the failure: the gods punish the presumptuous, as they punished Croesus in the sixth century B.C. and Pyrrhus in the third, who had asked the gods if they were right to enter into battle, the former with the Persians, the latter with the Romans. To each Apollo had replied that "by doing so the king would destroy a great empire," without specifying that it was the empire of the suppliant, not that of his adversary. Here again, the problem with oracles was not obtaining them, but understanding them.

It would be interesting to estimate the impact of Illous' revolt, not on the great families who daily saw themselves increasingly obliged to choose between fidelity to the cults and the possibility of a political career, but on the ordinary followers of paganism, the simple folk without ancestors and without power, who held on to their traditions no less stubbornly. The extent of the persecutions waged by John of Ephesus a century later provides the only index we have of their tenacity.

· 8 ·

Masters and Pupils, or the
Appeal of Paganism

AT the end of the fifth century only one area remained in which pagans could still exercise a degree of power: the liberal professions, teaching in particular. The very different examples of Hypatia and Pamprepius prove that one could not with impunity be both influential and at the same time marginal. (Much later, "court Jews" would often suffer the same bitter fate.) The faith of such pagans had long since become a private matter, and the secret practices that on discovery occasionally provoked a scandal had only private aims: to conceive a child, gain the love of an unattainable woman, find a treasure, secure a position, and so on. In such matters paganism maintained an indisputable appeal. Whenever we are able to catch glimpses of private lives, the gulf that the law persisted in widening between those in the right and those entrenched in error seems considerably narrowed.

Among all the many forms of pagan practices, divination and magic continued to be the overriding concern of the authorities. Although only the faithful understood the meaning of the cults, magic affected universal desires. A Christian author might well ridicule the soothsayer who predicted to the master of the household that his unborn child would be a boy, while saying to the old nanny, "It will be a girl, but I said a boy so as not to displease the master" (it was a girl).[1] Such ruses, which seem like student pranks, might also have proved useful to the worthy bishop of Gaza who promised the empress a boy. In apologetic accounts imposture characterizes an adversary, but miracles show the author's approval; the outcome condemns one and affirms the other. In daily life this distribution must have seemed less clear, and the mistakes of the pseudo-scientific astrologers must have been no more frequent than those of naively faithful hermits.

Proclus, the Heir

Pagans necessarily became men of learning rather than of action, as exemplified by Olympiodorus. And Athens, where he studied, became the refuge of "contemplative" paganism. For more than half a century Athens was distinguished by the presence of the philosopher Proclus, from 430–432 until his death on April 17, 485. Proclus arguably was one of the most appealing pagan figures of the fifth century, and one of the best known, thanks to the biography written by his disciple and successor, Marinus of Neapolis (Nablus, in Samaria). This biography, it must be admitted, is not always up to the intellectual level of the subject, who at twenty-eight wrote an extraordinary commentary on Plato's *Timaeus*.[2]

At Athens, Proclus spent his life in a small town that was filled with the most magnificent works of art of Greek civilization, but was politically and administratively insignificant (Corinth had replaced it centuries before) and had no particular resources outside of its teachers and schools. Proclus may have been preparing for an administrative career: he studied Latin in Alexandria and accompanied his master and the governor of Egypt to Constantinople. It was there that Athena appeared to him and revealed his true vocation, philosophy. After returning to Alexandria, and then settling in Athens, he spent his days in close contact with the gods who had guided him, especially Athena and Asclepius. He avoided men in power, except those at the lower echelon of Athenian municipal life; this was necessary to perfect his role of Sophist—representative and defender of his city.

Proclus' memorable sayings and deeds, preserved by his entourage and carefully selected and interpreted as so many symbols, would have him appear as the heir of a tradition that was threatened but not doomed. When he arrived in Athens, coming from the port of Piraeus to the city, the first water he drank was that which came from the spring in the sanctuary consecrated to Socrates. That same evening, at sundown, when he climbed to the gates of the Acropolis, the guardian who was about to leave said: "To tell the truth, had you not come, I would have locked up."

Within their small circle, even minor discomfitures were reinterpreted positively. We learn that a "storm," blown by "the breath of Typhonic winds" ("wind"and "spirit" are rendered by the same word in Greek), "contrary to a well-ruled life," compelled Proclus to spend one year away from Athens. Which kind of storm? Those "Typhonian spirits"—spreading trouble and confusion, like the monstrous Typhon, last and most dangerous of all Zeus's primitive foes—and those "Giants-vultures"—meaning probably "Giants [Sons of Mother Earth and menacing to Zeus] riding on vultures"— allude to the Christians, as has been shown by H. D. Saffrey.[3]

Marinus' words are scornful and violent, nevertheless he avoids naming his master's enemies more explicitly. Proclus' temporary exile is described by his pious biographer in a manner that is totally symbolic. Proclus has proved his ability to "swim his way through life," to "obey the universal revolving"—though the grand maritime circular travel resulted in a mere crossing of the Aegean to Lydia, a province of Asia Minor even closer to Athens than the philosopher's native Lycia was. There he discreetly had himself initiated into the local cults, and, when the opportunity arose, he reformed them, guided by his own knowledge or by divine intervention. In a place called Adrotta, otherwise unknown, people had forgotten whether the patron of the sanctuary was Asclepius the healer or the Dioscuri, protectors of seafarers. In a dream Proclus discovered that the two young men were in fact the two young sons of Asclepius, Machaon and Podalirius. The god appeared to him, asking: "Have you not heard Iamblichus tell who they are?" Proclus' solution not only avoided offending any of the divine powers that inhabited the place, it also received the sanction of a modern theurgist. Having thus, under the care of the gods, completed his experience of the traditional cults in a most conservative province, a wiser Proclus returned to Athens, where "Giants-vultures" were dozing.

Proclus was concerned that nothing be omitted from religious practices. He observed the rites of the cult of the Great Mother, said to be Phrygian but at that late date more at home among the aristocratic pagans in Rome than in the highlands of Phrygia. He celebrated such non-Greek gods as Marnas of Gaza, Asclepius Master of the Lions of Ascalon, Theandrites the Arabian god, and Isis of Philae, in Upper Egypt. Thanks to his great knowledge of magic, he worked wonders, ending a drought and moving away earth tremors with his amulets. Asclepius worked miraculous recoveries when he sought help on behalf of his master's daughter and relieved Proclus' arthritis of the knee.[4] This universal initiate, schooled in Orphic as well as Chaldaean doctrines, teaches us a great deal about the beliefs and rituals of late paganism. His conduct as a "man of god" was quite unusual, however, and his influence was limited to a very narrow circle.

In this respect, beyond the contrast between his shining intelligence, his active temperament, and the marginality of his life, what is most typical about him may be his origins. His parents were from Xanthus (now Günük) in Lycia, on the southwestern coast of Asia Minor. In the course of this chapter we shall meet a number of students, many of them pagans, from the same region that in the previous century produced Chrysanthius and his disciple Eunapius of Sardis. It was, however, in Alexandria and in Beirut, where seemingly there was more preparation for public life than in Athens, that they were active, as shown in an account which has come down to us intact.

The Return to Alexandria

This account, which takes us into late fifth-century society where pagans and Christians mingled freely, is the *Life of Severus* related by Zacharias the Scholastic, from Maiouma, Severus' friend and fellow disciple. Severus, born in Asia Minor at Sozopolis in Pisidia, became patriarch of Antioch. Being from the anti-Chalcedonian party, and not having been baptized as an infant, he was accused by his enemies of paganism. They found him too cultivated, too brilliant, not to have consorted with the demons during his youth. What was more, he had studied not only in Alexandria but in Beirut, a city where queer relations were inevitable. To clear Severus of these calumnies Zacharias undertook to relate his life, laying particular stress on the relations of his hero in his youth with pagan students in the liberal arts (*eleutheroi diatribai*) and the law.[5] Zacharias was an eyewitness to the incidents he relates, which took place in Alexandria in 485–487 and in Beirut in 487–491. He brings to life—with detail and, one may expect, with accuracy—a vigorous, agitated academic world that was cut off neither from the provinces from which its members originated, nor from the major cities that received them.[6]

Severus came from a Christian background. His grandfather was the bishop of his native city. From the mountains of Pisidia, one need only go down to the coast for the winds to carry one directly to Alexandria, the great metropolis "on the edge of Egypt." It is there that Severus began his studies in rhetoric, balancing his readings in Libanius with the works of the rhetor's correspondent, Basil the Cappodocian saint. In Alexandria, Severus joined with other young men from good Asia Minor families. Among them was Paralius, a pagan from Aphrodisias in Caria, whose story, related in detail by Zacharias, allows us to witness the process of a conversion, while at the same time introducing major well-known figures in Alexandria's pagan community .

Paralius studied with the grammarian Horapollo, who "knew his art extremely well and whose teaching was worthy of great praise; but he was a pagan, and filled with admiration for demons and magic." Although at the start he shared his master's ideas, Paralius abandoned them. Two experiences contributed to this change of heart. In the first place, one of his brothers had previously come to Alexandria, where he converted to Christianity, even becoming a monk. Conversations with that brother began to shake Paralius' convictions, and the replies he received from his Neoplatonist masters to the objections he brought them from the monastery did little to quell his doubts. The second experience had to do with a barren woman from Aphrodisias, married to an Alexandrian, who went with her husband to consult Isis in a semi-clandestine temple that still stood in the area of Canopus, at Menouthis.

Canopus, famous from the time Alexandria was founded, was a resort on the coast, 15 miles east of Alexandria (today near Abukir). To go there by boat along the canal was a delight both because of the site and for the monuments (among them, the temple of Aphrodite on Cape Zephyrion); one went for pleasure and for faith. Near the end of the fourth century a pagan holy man, Antoninus, who had found shelter there from the disturbances of Alexandria, attracted devotees. In 414 Bishop Cyril had the famous sanctuary of Isis at Menouthis laid waste; the building then received the relics of the Holy Cyr and John. Isis' cult, expelled from its true home, had to find an emergency refuge—the crypt of some other temple, it would seem—where it was able to continue for another seventy years.

After the region was completely christianized, the church of the Evangelists continued to be a much frequented place of pilgrimage and prophecy. The faithful continued to sleep in the sanctuary, hoping for dreams of salvation. In the closing years of the fifth century Isis worked her last miracle: she provided a child for the barren couple. The priestess did not make the woman fertile but gave the couple her own child. This story about a child provided through secret adoption, utterly unremarkable in Antiquity, was presented by believers as a miracle worked by their goddess. Incredulous Christians advised Paralius to have an honest woman verify whether his compatriot had any milk, for this would be the proof of her having given birth. The philosophers rejected any verification.[7]

Paganism thus admitted its lack of credibility with regard to dogma (in the conversations Paralius held with monks and philosophers) and with regard to miracles (the pilgrimage of the sterile couple to Menouthis). The final blow was delivered by the demon itself. While Paralius was sleeping in Menouthis (in the sanctuary, in order to consult the oracle through dreams), Isis commanded him "to beware of [another pupil of Horapollo], who is a magician." She told the same thing to the other pupil about Paralius. When Paralius begged her to reveal what was going on, she remained mute and refused to appear to him, despite all the sacrifices he offered her. This attempt to estrange him from his fellow pupils, before disappearing as though she were discouraged—doubt cast by the goddess herself on the value of practices presumed to honor her—ultimately discredited Isis in Paralius' eyes. He turned instead to "the Lord, creator of the heavens." This is a remarkable formula, for it had never before sufficed to invoke only one god. The Neoplatonists would have entirely agreed that

God, in his many manifestations, is one. But what is unique about the God of the Jews and the Christians is that he is the creator of the universe, which pagans regarded as not created.[8]

From then on Paralius ridiculed the "orgies of the priestess of Isis," whom he now saw as nothing but a prostitute. One day Paralius' fellow students took advantage of their teacher's absence to give the apostate a thrashing. He was saved just in time by the Christian students. The case went before the prefect, who received the agitated students and monks very coolly—which was enough to make the pious author of the *Life of Severus* accuse him of paganism. If the case was played down in court, in the street it was amplified into a riot that turned into a wholesale persecution of pagans. The most influential fled, among them Horapollo, although Zacharias' account absolves him since Paralius had been attacked in his absence.[9]

This incident led to the devastation of the last sanctuary of Isis in Menouthis. The bishop of Alexandria organized a raid, led by Paralius, of clerics and monks from a monastery in Canopus. The celebrants of the sanctuary had walled up the entrance to the chamber of the pagan images, camouflaging it with a piece of furniture. But in front of it, in full daylight, a lamp burned, and incense and sweets were set out. Did the pagans hope to cheat their persecutors by exhibiting a rather harmless domestic altar, suggesting that there was nothing more to discover? Paralius, momentarily confused, soon uncovered the ruse; the entrance was reopened; and a monk from Canopus, a native Egyptian, entered the hiding place.

Most of the images seem to have been made of wood and were small enough to be passed to those outside by one person. They had been salvaged from the Iseum in Memphis, ancient pharaonic capital of the north, from which the celebrant of the temple had taken them "when it became evident that paganism had lost its hold and was being abolished." This may refer, if not to an earlier date, at the latest to the years of despondency that followed the laws of Theodosius I in 391 and 392 as well as the destruction of the Alexandrian Serapeum. It also doubtless reflects a local situation in Memphis: the faithful were no longer numerous enough to assure the continuity of the cult and the safety of its statues, which had been moved closer to the great Greek city and to a safer place. But their fate had merely been delayed. In 486 some of those statues were burned in Menouthis; others, placed in an outbuilding of the church before their destruction the following day, were guarded by monks and Alexandrians who steeled themselves by singing canticles throughout the night. As for the Christians of Menouthis, all but the priest were terrified. The pagans of the small town waited in vain for their gods to confound the infidels. At daybreak, how relieved was one camp, how disappointed the other![10]

The next day the abode of the pagan statues was completely razed down to its foundations, as was usual for the lairs of "false gods," and a vast rampage was unleashed. Monks and zealous laymen (*philoponoi*) returned to Alexandria with the pagan priest from Menouthis, whom they had arrested, along with twenty camels laden with idols. In the capital the mob brought together quantities of statues found in the baths and in private homes—not all of them cult idols, to be sure. They broke the legs and arms of the idols, shouting, "their gods do not have surgeons!" Everything was piled on a pyre in a public square. Descriptions of this scene speak of Egyptian gods with animal bodies: dogs (Anubis), monkeys (Thoth), cats (Bastet), all except for a "Kronos" (Sobek the crocodile) whose statue was "filled with blood." Thanks to this so-called Kronos (the same as Saturn, the god who devoured his own children), the hiding place revealed the true nature of pagan gods: impotent ogres.

Among their insults, the mob called them by Greek names—Kronos, Zeus, Dionysus, Athena, Artemis, Ares, Apollo—which are not the usual Greek equivalents of the indigenous deities. The people, or the author who speaks for them, merely repeated the invectives of the Church Fathers against the immorality of paganism, those gods who drank, copulated promiscuously, and delighted in killing mortals. The pagan priest was forced to tell the name and explain the attributes and appearance of each of the divinities before they were destroyed. Zacharias does not seem to have been particularly interested in this detail, intended to demean the prohibited cults. First came the snake, "the one that fooled Eve." Which god was that? Among the many snakes that appear in the divine world of ancient Egypt, we might rather think of the Agathos Daimon, the Good Genius so popular in late Alexandria.[11]

Turning from statues to people, the author does not reveal the fate of the priest, who was subject to death. Since Horapollo had fled, the populace had to content itself with jeering at his name, calling him not "Horapollo" but "Psychapollo," killer of souls. He later converted, under no constraint, as Damascius related with sadness, and perhaps even some bitterness. This conversion was not an immediate result of the "Paralius case," for in a document written under the reign of Anastasius (491–518), Horapollo still uses a formula with a discreet but distinct pagan flavor. He was in contention with his cousin-german, a childhood friend whom he had married and who had fled with a lover, stripping the family home of all its furnishings. Horapollo appealed to the court to prevent her from seizing real estate as well. In the legal formula of the oath, he swears "in the name of the all-powerful God," using an epithet more suited to an Alexandrian philosopher than the "creator of the heavens" invoked by Paralius when he espoused Christianity.[12] With or without Horapollo, a scandal like this necessarily carried in its wake a rash of conversions.

The group of intellectuals mentioned by Zacharias—specifically Horapollo, Asclepiodotus, Heraiscus, Ammonius, and Isidorus—reappears in the *Life of Isidorus* by Damascius. It is tempting to assume that the scuffles with the police mentioned in the fragments of the work that have been preserved are related to the same period.[13] Tempting, but not certain, since according to those fragments, the police investigated a group around Ammonius, not Horapollo, and some of the figures are different. On the pagan side, the professor of Greek, Harpocras, and on the Christian side, the police officer, Nicomedes, are not mentioned in the *Life of Severus*. Furthermore, in this account, Horapollo and his uncle Heraiscus were arrested and whipped, but did not reveal the whereabouts of Harpocras and Ammonius. The two episodes cannot be fused, and circumstances in the one related by Damascius are more difficult for us to grasp than in the other, because of the fragmentation of Damascius' work. Ammonius, who appears in Damascius as the prime target of the authorities, is accused by the philosopher of having reached an agreement with the bishop in order to continue teaching.[14]

And should we conclude from Zacharias' account that "Horapollo's lectures were a school of fanaticism"? Once again, the pagans seem to be on the defensive when confronted by the zeal of the Christians, who had become the unbeaten victors of the streets and the watchdogs of any suspicious behavior—in this case, the machinations of a couple in search of a child. In Alexandria, a century after the Theodosian laws and the destruction of the Serapeum, a cult with little remaining but magic tricks finally raised doubts among its own adherents. A mere handful by then, they became suspicious of one another, waiting in anguish for the moment when that last remaining bastion of active gods, its powers exhausted, would also fall silent.

Beirut the Beautiful

The atmosphere in Beirut was very different and much more salubrious for its pagan inhabitants, who found greater sympathy both in the city itself and in the surrounding hillside. In the Bekaa Valley, whose port Beirut can be considered, there were no concentrations of monks but rather masses of peasants still faithful to the old beliefs. Beirut, famous for its schools of Roman law, was a great and prosperous city that received its statute of metropolis in August 409.[15] Because of its location, climate, and environs, it was also a resort, a "source of pleasures" (*hēdonôn pēgē*), unlike Alexandria, "where orthodoxy has always reigned."[16] Beirut seems to have had no bishops of the caliber of an Athanasius or a Cyril of Alexandria. In 470, a few decades before Severus and Zacharias came to live in Beirut, the Egyptian poet Nonnus of Panopolis drew a flattering portrait of it in his *Dionysiaca*, calling it Beroe:

> Beroe, root of life, nursemaid of cities, glory of kings,
> First to appear, born with Time, old as the universe,
> Dwelling of Hermes, seat of Justice, city of Laws,
> Home of Joy, palace of the Paphian, house of Love,
> Delectable sojourn of Bacchus, territory of the Archeress,
> Trophy of the Nereides, castle of Zeus, court of Ares,
> Dancing ground of the Graces, star of the land of Lebanon,
> As old as Tethys, as heavy with years as Ocean
> Who engendered Beroe.[17]

In this litany, beginning and ending with an encomium of Beirut's antiquity, the mythological allusions convey the image of a city of law courts (line 3) and pleasures (line 4, "the Paphian" being Aphrodite), of countryside (line 5), vineyards (line 5, "sojourn of Bacchus"), and forests for hunting (line 5, "territory of the Archeress (Artemis)." It is also, as one can see from reading the entire excerpt, a city where the ancient gods were still at home.

This may explain the itinerary of John, called the Fuller, originally from Thebes in Egypt, who, as his name indicates, was born a Christian. Attracted to the cult of demons in the hope that they would give him the woman he loved but could not win, he took up permanent residence in Beirut. His was not what he would consider a true conversion. John the Fuller did not adopt a faith that he regarded as superior to his own. He indulged for a specific purpose in practices that his morality surely condemned. Along with accomplices, he had even been on the point of immolating a black slave in the circus at midnight. Disturbed by passersby at the crucial moment, the magicians fled and the liberated victim denounced their plan. But instead of being brought to trial, John the Fuller was discreetly admonished by his former coreligionists, and in 490 rejoined "the true faith" with no other punishment than having to attend church services with his mentors for some period of time, in tearful and profound repentance.[18] We may infer that he desisted from hoping that the fair woman would bestow her favors upon him.

This event caused the city's pagans a great deal of trouble. The names John revealed to his admonishers, and the denunciation by a copyist who had been given a book on magic to copy for one of the same people, enabled Zacharias and his friends to lodge a complaint before the bishop without compromising John. The books of two of the accused were seized and burned; the other accused took their books with them when they fled. There was some kind of civic strife, as part of the population of Beirut sided with the pagans—gangs Zacharias describes as including assassins and prostitutes.[19] On the other hand, a great Christian landowner brought into town squads of his peasants ready to strike down every pagan they laid hands on. Less fanatical Christian plaintiffs managed, not without difficulty, to rescue their professor, Leontius, from the peasants. He then left Beirut and naturally became a convert.

Among the pagans exposed by this episode, two figures emerge in some detail: Leontius and Chrysaorius. Leontius taught "preliminary science," which for a Christian would be the philosophy necessary to prepare for a true understanding of religion.[20] But on the side he read horoscopes, "and led [his clients] to have recourse to idols."[21] It is surely of him that Damascius writes: "Leontius, who thought he had worked out a marvelous solution, returned to his home with a license to speak that was both unfortunate and ill-starred. He achieved neither the fortune nor the security he hoped for, and lost the piety that makes one beloved of God, thereby irremediably destroying his soul." This peevish and ineffectual excommunication conveys to us that Leontius, because of his past, had some problems later on, if, as seems likely, Damascius is speaking of the same individual.[22]

Chrysaorius remained in Beirut, where some time later he fell victim to a swindle over hidden treasure. "Vagabonds and magicians" promised to uncover treasure once upon a time hidden by the great Darius, king of Persia. They asked for "silver objects," which were required "by one group, in order to go to the sea nearby and to summon the demons, guardians of the treasure, with those objects; and, by the other, to practice necromancy in the tombs within the temple [a Christian funerary church]."

Chrysaorius gave the church guardian, himself an accomplice, the silver objects for the sorcerers at the seaside, who disappeared after a few charades on the beach, as well as a censer for the necromancer. But just as he was about to coerce the souls of the dead to reveal the hiding place of the treasure, a seismic shock frightened and betrayed the desecrators, for it awakened the indigent people sleeping in the church.[23]

The paganism that emerges from these anecdotes is pretty shoddy, a religion for status-losing persons or mere secret sorcery: books on magic, like those of John the Fuller, hidden in the false bottom of a chair; human sacrifices in the circus, theft and profanation of sacred vases; necromancy. True or not, such charges foreshadow the Middle Ages. As for the moves made by Christians toward pagan practices, their far from disinterested forays into their neighbor's back yard are of little consequence.

The Two Faces of Gaza

Far more significant for the future was the Christian absorption of pagan culture. It took place of course in the capital, Constantinople, but found more fertile ground elsewhere. Constantinople, even after five chairs of Greek rhetoric and three of Latin had been established there by Theodosius II in 425, was still unimportant as a center. Antioch, former capital of Greek culture and mother city of Libanius, played a major role. It attained celebrity because one of the students of the great professor Theodorus, who was the bishop of Mopsuestia from 390 to 428, applied to the Bible the methods employed for the criticism and exegesis of pagan texts.

But above all it was Gaza, not so long ago a bastion of paganism, that became a center of Christian teaching of rhetoric, thanks to one of its natives, Procopius. We know neither where nor under whom he was trained, but if it was not in his native city then perhaps, like his colleague, compatriot, and contemporary Aeneas, he studied in Alexandria. Procopius was a cleric, versed in theology, who knew Plato well and argued with Proclus. He was the inventor of "exegetic chains," a method of commenting upon sacred authors that consisted of compiling earlier commentaries, listed under the name of their author, with the compiler proving his cleverness merely by a judicious choice of texts.[24]

Procopius also wrote on secular subjects. Alongside paraphrases of Homer, he described the astronomical clock in the market square of Gaza. This reflects the taste of the times for automatons and mechanisms. But what interested Procopius was not the mechanism of the clock, but rather the effect it produced, the animation of its mythological decorations: Hercules accomplishing his twelve labors in the course of the twelve hours; the Sun on its rounds; and minor figures such as Pan and a Diomede playing the trumpet. These figures, at least the first two, are not merely fictional characters. Hercules and especially the Sun occupied a primordial place in the pagan beliefs of Late Antiquity. Furthermore, given the proximity of astrology and astronomy, it is often difficult to separate one strand from the other, as has been seen in connection with Theon, Hypatia's father.[25]

Procopius, the sincerity of whose piety cannot be doubted, must have believed that he was treating worldly subjects whose local application carried more weight than any implication of impiety. This is true also of his description of Aphrodite and Adonis—inseparable from the "festival of Roses," the *Rosalia*—who appeared on the mosaics that decorated a building in his city.[26] Procopius was evidently from an important Gaza family. One of his brothers was named "governor of the islands" (of the Aegean). Another, a lawyer of the imperial court, supported a request from Gaza to the prefect of the Praetorium. Procopius himself applied his pen to celebrate the beauties of their little homeland. As for the outcome of his teaching, one can understand why in the tenth century the patriarch Photius grumbled on reading what one of Procopius' disciples wrote: "He is devoted to the true religion; he respects the rites and sacred places of Christians. Nonetheless, for whatever reason of negligence or thoughtlessness, he mixes into his writings ill-suited pagan fables and stories, at times even when treating sacred subjects."[27]

The disciple in question, Choricius, discloses, in a *Defense of Actors*, his familiarity with classical theater, particularly that of Menander. In principle, the Church condemned the production of plays as a kind of complicity in adultery. But this did not prevent the continuation of performances in daring forms, which another Procopius, from Caesarea, described when relating the theatrical debut of the future empress, Theodora, wife of Justinian, in what we would regard today as pornography. The theater defended by Choricius was more dignified than that, but it was similar.[28]

The School of Gaza demonstrates how Christians garnered from paganism more than insipid literary ornaments: Victories brandishing the palm frond; plump-cheeked Cupids holding garlands aloft; Seasons tendering the fruits and flowers of the year. What we see surviving are the entertainments that reflect the image of a society, so artfully captured by Menander eight hundred years earlier that the first Byzantines still recognized themselves in his plays. They also reflect local traditions, the pride of cities that still provided the strength and prosperity of the Empire. Though increasingly distorted, those traditions survived in a Christian environment. In sixth-century Antioch, the work of John Malalas (Malalas means "rhetor" in Syriac) serves as an outstanding example.[29] We might also include John the Lydian.

Gaza, a prosperous city, the hub of trading with the East, found particularly burdensome the tax that merchants had to pay the imperial treasury every five years, the *chrysargyros*. Remember that Honorius congratulated himself on the moneys that came to him from that city, which during his time was still pagan. The revocation of the *chrysargyros* in 498 by Emperor Anastasius was hailed by Gaza's men of letters, no matter what their religious bent: the rhetor Procopius, the poet Timotheus, and the last pagan historian whose works have been preserved, a pupil of Procopius, Zosimus, who held the title of count and had formerly been a lawyer for the Treasury.[30]

It is interesting to compare Olympiodorus and Zosimus. The former wrote at the time of the restoration of the Western Empire, which was to be its last. By the time of the latter, seventy or eighty years later, the West was lost. Whereas Olympiodorus ended his account in 425, Zosimus stopped in 410, just before Rome was sacked by Alaric. In keeping with traditional historiography, he must have intended to bring his chronicle up to the death of the reigning emperor's predecessor, that is, Zeno's death in 491.[31] The fact that he did not tells us something. Seen with hindsight, 410 had become a decisive turning point. Zosimus, as compared for example with Rutilius Namatianus who had left Rome a few years after 410, was aware of the decline of the Roman Empire. He had no trouble explaining it: Christianity was to blame—an accusation with little foundation, but destined to have a very long future.

• • •

THE last pagans we can see clearly are to be found mainly among intellectuals, historians, philosophers, and poets. Some seem to have been genuinely taken with pagan theology. Such a one was Nonnus of Panopolis, who had a Christian name, and who wrote a vast mythological epic, the *Dionysiaca*. Into that work he inserted a hymn to Hercules-Sun, divine king of Tyre, which cannot readily pass for a mere literary exercise. This pagan sensibility, these meditations that had to take their inspiration from contact with a site presumed to hold some remnant of what had been sacred, can also be found in Asclepiodotus of Aphrodisias, a contemporary of Nonnus but of pagan background, who went to the sanctuary of Apollo of the Valleys as a pilgrim, or, a generation later, in Simplicius, a pilgrim to the springs of Khabur in northern Mesopotamia, about 53 miles east of Harran.[32]

This kind of paganism could not have survived without the existence of a pagan population large enough to protect the sacred character of those places, and discreet enough not to attract the wrath of the authorities. Although extirpated from the public domain by the laws of Theodosius I, paganism maintained a secret vitality in the hearts and souls of individuals.

· 9 ·

The Fragmented West

AT the end of the fifth century the difference between the two former halves of the Empire was striking, at least with regard to the cities. While the Mediterranean East was rather prosperous, the West was collapsing; centuries would pass before it recovered. By admonishing his flock in 494 not to try to recover by superstition the prosperity that the East was enjoying without any lapse of faith, Pope Gelasius was in fact acknowledging the reality of the divergence. Gelasius lived during what we regard as "the awkward age" of Western culture, before Boethius restored its luster for a few years (507–524) in Ravenna, and before Saint Benedict founded the monastery at Monte Cassino in 529—the very year Justinian ordered the closing of the Platonist school of Athens. This is too striking a coincidence to be overlooked, but its significance should not be overestimated. No torch passed at that time from East to West; night did not fall on one side as dawn rose on the other.

The Time of Soothsayers

Throughout most of the fifth century pagans were as uncommon in the political forefront in the West as in the East, and we know little about those who chanced to have any real power. In 455 Genseric, who came from Carthage with his Vandals, conquered Rome and sacked it for two weeks. A Roman of good family named Marcellinus, master of Dalmatia from 454 to 468, led the struggle against the Vandals and recaptured Sardinia and Sicily. Marcellinus was regarded as a devout pagan, watchful for heavenly signs and an expert in divination. In 468, during a campaign in Sicily, he was treacherously assassinated by his Roman allies, which led the king of the Vandals to say that "the Romans had cut their right hand with their left."[1]

Marcellinus' assassination can be explained by the power and autonomy he had acquired, apart from his religious beliefs. His nephew Nepos, who succeeded him, was a Christian, whereas his murderer would seem to have been inclined toward paganism. Nepos sat briefly on the throne of Rome (474–475) before retiring to Dalmatia, after which Odoacer, master of Italy, used his name to give imperial legitimacy to the coins he struck. This was the period of the last rulers of the Western Empire.

Marcellinus was said to be a soothsayer. This same allegation was leveled against Eucherius, the son of Stilico, scion of a Christian family. The paganism of these generals and statesmen was not always related to a family or ethnic tradition (we have no details about Marcellinus' family), but often came from an attraction to pagan wisdom. This was true of Marcellinus who was a friend of the philosopher Sallustius. At first glance, Sallustius seems to have been eccentric, judging by his provocative attitude which "turned young people away from philosophy," either through aversion toward those who were teaching it, or because Sallustius discouraged them by presenting philosophy as an enterprise for which no man is worthy enough. But this was only a method of testing the pupil to ascertain the seriousness of his intentions. Four centuries earlier it had been employed by Musonius Rufus, the teacher of Epictetus.[2] What particularly interested those personages who held positions as precarious as they were elevated was soothsaying, and always for the same reasons: it served to seize and maintain power; it was a science of government. Even Marcellinus may have practiced it. Others resorted to horoscopes, as did Illous in the East with Pamprepius.

Anthemius, emperor of the West though of Greek origin, who so rashly had disposed of Marcellinus, was also considered a pagan by Damascius. This was because he had arrived from the East attended by a Roman, Messus Phoebus Severus, who, disillusioned with public service in his own city, had retired to Alexandria to study. If Anthemius was a pagan, it was only within the secrecy of his conscience. He was born into a Christian family and never publicly disclaimed his religion. In the eyes of his Western subjects he was a Greek, a *Hellene*, which was enough to make him suspect. As for Severus, his horse emitted bursts of sparks when curried, which presaged a brilliant future for the master. Severus in fact became consul in 470, after which time the omen ceased.[3] Pagans came close to the throne only in connection with divinatory rites, which would cease when the throne remained vacant, a time that was fast approaching.

The paganism that lingered on in what remained of Roman political institutions increasingly seems to have been reduced to superstitious practices or to mere respect for relics of the past. Efforts made at the time to preserve some statues should not be understood as a propagan position. Stilico, though a devout Christian, was not opposed to the presence of the statue of Victory in the Curia.[4] At the end of the century restorations, or false attributions of works to famous masters such as Phidias or Polycletes to protect them from vandalism, stemmed from the same attitude.[5] At the time of Odoacer and Theodoric the Senate resumed striking coins, like those with

Romulus and Remus on the face, and the she-wolf on the back, with the overly optimistic motto *Roma Invicta*, "Invincible Rome."[6] As Peter Brown has said, pagan roots remained constantly present. But by then they were feeding professions of faith that were purely political and perfectly compatible with Christianity. The "Catholic and apostolic" Church, which is to say "universal and proselytizing," was also "Roman."

One cannot trust any isolated allegation about the pagan beliefs of so-and-so, whoever the author, whether made by its adherents or its adversaries. We have seen this at Constantinople, in connection with Cyrus, and, in the West, on the subject of Eucherius (accused like Cyrus by political enemies), or the emperor Anthemius (to whom Damascius attributed a most improbable paganism). The laws of exclusion from the beginning of the century, by permitting scurrilous charges to flourish, make it hard to know who really was a pagan and what it meant to be one.

The Time of Kings

By the end of the fifth century the Western Empire had crumbled. The emperors who followed one another rapidly on the Western throne after Anthemius' assassination in 472 either came from the Dalmatian refuge of Salona (Split), Diocletian's city, or retired there: Glycerius, Nepos, Romulus, the child enthroned by his father, Orestes. In 476 Odoacer deposed Romulus and reigned until 490, at first under the nominal authority of Nepos (killed in 480).

In another period Odoacer, son of one of Attila's guards, would have held the title of commander in chief, *magister utriusque militiae*, the post Alaric coveted before 410. In 476, after making himself chief of the tribes that formed the bulwark of the Roman army in Italy and promising them lands, he became their king. This was also the period when Clovis became king of the Franks (481 or 482 until 511), and cut a vast domain for them out of what had previously been Gaul. In 488, from the East, Zeno sent Theodoric, who was also a Roman general and had been consul, against Odoacer, king of the Ostrogoths. Theodoric encircled Odoacer in Ravenna, where he held him under siege for three years. He reigned in Italy until his death in 526, without having obtained from Zeno's successor, Anastasius, the title of Emperor of the West. He had to content himself with being king of the Goths. Anastasius, recognizing the power of Clovis, granted him the title of honorary consul. If the king of the Franks was proclaimed Augustus, meaning emperor, it was only by an assembly of the people of Touraine, devoid of any but local significance.[7] To this picture, already muddled by fragmentation, we must add the Vandals in Africa, the Visigoths in Spain and Aquitaine, and the Burgundians in what would become Burgundy.

To be sure, religion had a role to play here, but not pagan religions. All but one of the tribes had been converted to Arian Christianity before they came into the Roman Empire. The Franks remained faithful to their Germanic cults until they embraced Catholicism, after Christ, invoked by Clovis during a battle against the Alamans, once more gave proof of his military ability. (Long afterward this episode would be used to rouse the spirits of the "Franks" of the Third Republic when faced with the "Alamans" of the Second Reich.) Classical paganism, linked with an imperial power that no longer existed, had no place in the new world.

Rome would never again be the political capital of an empire. In the sixth century, in 536 and the years following, Rome was fought over by the Byzantines commanded by Belisarius and the Goths. When, in 552, Narses, Belisarius' successor, finally triumphed over "Totila the wily," king of the Goths, and recaptured Rome, the city was in complete decline—ruined, impoverished, deserted.

An Absence of Pagans

The West had been one of the cradles of late pagan beliefs. Was it not in Rome that, under Gallienus (253–268), Plotinus (died 270) taught and found an audience among the aristocracy, and in Rome and Sicily that Porphyry wrote (died ca. 301–305)? Plotinus' influence was felt earlier in these regions than in the Hellenic world. But in the fourth century the only pagan Latin writers who seem to have known Porphyry's work—Marius Victorinus or Firmicus Maternus—converted to Christianity. Firmicus Maternus, who wrote a treatise on astrology while still a pagan and, after his conversion, a pamphlet on *The Error of Pagan Religions* (around 346), had little influence on the thinking of his time.[8] This was not true of Marius Victorinus, who passed Neoplatonism on to Augustine.[9] In Rome at the end of the century Christians were the readers and users of Plotinus and Porphyry. "The true successor [of those writers] as mentor to the Roman nobility was Saint Jerome."[10]

A quiet paganism emerges from some of the little poems collected by Naucellius, a friend of Symmachus, at the end of the fourth century. It is the same tone as the epigram in which Ampelius, proconsul of Achaia, had celebrated a half-century earlier the park he had made for him in Aegina: "And here I take all my pleasures and delight in them: countryside, villa, gardens watered by natural springs, and the lovely marbles of the odd-numbered Pierians [nine Muses]. Here I want to stay and live out a serene old age, re-reading the sage texts of the Ancients."[11]

The taste of these people for a certain kind of culture was not without ostentation. They also enjoyed the traditional feasts and honors that are described in *Against the Pagans*, a poem composed in the wake of an attempted restoration of paganism and a failed coup, hard to date—it could have been 385 (Maximus), 394 (Eugenius), or 408–409 (Attalus).[12] The rituals described—a prefect holding the silver reins of a chariot drawn by lions, on which Cybele makes her entrance into the city—are more congruous with the period 384–393 than the tragic years of 408–409. In 408–409 the prefect Gabinius Barbarus Pompeianus could no longer conduct public ceremonies.[13] Customs or nostalgia therefore lingered on in ways suggested by the priest of Marseilles, Salvian who, in his book *On the Government of God* written in the 440s, expressed outrage over the fact that the consuls continued to read auguries and feed the sacred chickens.[14]

On the whole, however, the generation that followed Eugenius' aborted coup (394) observed the progressive conversion of Roman aristocracy with neither distress nor rejection. In 431 the grandson of Virius Nicomachus Flavianus—the pagan spirit behind that revolt, who committed suicide after his defeat—raised a statue to his forebear, "on the emperor's orders."[15] Christianized nobles preserved Roman traditions. Not only did Christianity tolerate their national pride, it offered them a new manifestation of it when Pope Leo I "the Great" (440–461), conferring on Rome the praise attributed to the Jewish people, glorified "a holy nation, a chosen people, a priestly and royal city" (*gens sancta, populus electus, civitas sacerdotalis et regia*).[16]

On the other hand, Leo rebuked the Christians who worshiped the rising sun on the steps of Saint Peter. The apse of the great basilica does in fact face west. In the atrium before the church some of the faithful prayed facing east, thus turning their backs on the tomb of the apostle. Leo's rebuke may have been directed toward former believers in the sun cult, or Manichaeans whose conversion to Christianity was not genuine. But the explanation proposed by the great exegete of ancient Christian rituals, Franz-Josef Dölger, may be the most suitable: Christian believers wanted to give a Christian meaning to a gesture of pagan origin which they restored, as did Manichaeans and others. This does not mean that they were crypto-pagans or crypto-Manichaeans. The custom apparently persisted as late as 1300, and Dölger compares it to Saint Francis' hymn to the sun: "Praise be to you, oh God my Lord, and to all your creatures, and above all to their great brother the sun, who brings the day and illumines with his light; and he is beautiful and brilliantly radiant; he is the symbol of you, oh Lord."[17]

In 494 Pope Gelasius prevented the Christian senator Andromachus from celebrating the Lupercalia. As Andromachus saw it, along with other Romans, Christians all, that February (*februarius*) holiday was supposed to halt the "fever" (*febris*) raging at the time. The pope pointed out to him that the true purpose of the holiday was to promote the fertility of women, that it was nothing more than a spectacle of licentious dances in which respectable matrons would not participate, that it was moreover ineffectual, and that the East, whose prosperity he contrasted with the misery of Italy, never celebrated it. Gelasius informs us that another devotion, to the Dioscuri, protectors of navigation, had also persisted. For the moment his arguments prevailed; nonetheless, the masquerades of February survived, in Rome and throughout Western civilization, all the way to the present.[18]

Strictly speaking, documents of this kind would not come under discussion in a history of the end of paganism. They bear witness to an attempt to purify the Christian faith and reveal merely one aspect of the complex, intimate, and often antagonistic relationship between Catholicism and classical secular culture. Those men, whom their bishop considered "neither pagans nor Christians," in my view were Christians who did not question their faith. Gelasius' policies would be pursued and extended up to the end of the sixth century, when Gregory the Great wrote Didier, bishop of Vienne: "A rumor has reached us, which we cannot repeat without embarrassment: your fraternity would seem to be teaching grammar to certain persons."[19]

The Citadel of Letters

In the Latin West of the fifth century literature provided paganism with a safer refuge than did ritualistic vestiges. I shall not discuss the *Historia Augusta*, a series of biographies of Roman emperors which succeeded those by Suetonius, and went from Nerva to Numerian (Diocletian's predecessor). These biographies, attributed to six different authors from the period of Diocletian and Constantine, may well have been written, and were assuredly edited, after 395, by a single author who was a confirmed pagan. Many uncertainties hang over these texts; it is far too difficult to sort out authentic documents from false ones, and to reveal the intentions they conceal.[20]

Macrobius offers a clearer voice. He probably wrote his *Saturnalia* shortly after 431, if not between 425 and 428, at any rate later than has been thought.[21] In spite of what Alan Cameron says, the work is not solely an idealized and nostalgic portrait of that which no longer existed. Like that of Nonnus, the work contains elements of solar theology, presented in a long speech that the author places in the mouth of a venerable champion of paganism, Vettius Agorius Praetextatus, who had died some fifty years earlier (in 384). "It could scarcely have occurred to Macrobius' Christian readers (by the 430s there would have been few pagan readers left) that there was anything anti-Christian about them," says Alan Cameron.[22] But did Macrobius have the option to enter into a polemic if he wished his book to escape the fate accorded Porphyry's treatise *Against Christians*—the pyre?

It is hard to see what interest Praetextatus' speech could have had unless it were seen from a pagan religious viewpoint. This is not a case of propaganda aimed at the outside world, but rather a theological meditation, a celebration that owes as much to poetry as to the writings of the philosophers. Praetextatus' only weapon against triumphant Christianity was silence, as Gaston Boissier justly observed.[23] Virgil, considered a *pontifex maximus*, has an important place in the *Saturnalia*, as he does in the *Commentary on Scipio's Dream* by the same author. The commentary devoted to him by the grammarian Servius, a bit older than Macrobius and from the same milieu, also stresses the religious significance of his work.[24] The *Saturnalia* begin with discussions of the calendar and feast days, immediately preceding the section on solar theology that concludes Book I. These are not meaningless topics. In the East a century later John of Lydia—as evidenced by his book *The Months*—is concerned with the same kind of etymologies that strike us as absurd and that in Macrobius are intimately related to astral beliefs inspired by Porphyry.[25] The beliefs have vanished but the fascination remains. Theurgy, however, held no interest for Macrobius, who did not find in his faith the practical applications that a Proclus of Athens found in his.

The best symbol of the transfer of a heritage that was both Greek and pagan to Latin-speaking Christians, and through them to new nations, is perhaps that found in the figure of the bishop of Clermont, Sidonius Apollinaris, who was born around 430 and died between 480 and 490. Sidonius, an admirer of Neoplatonist philosophy, revised the Latin translation of the *Life of Apollonius of Tyana* made a century before by the pagan aristocrat Nicomachus Flavianus, who committed suicide after Eugenius' defeat.[26] This was a work much appreciated by Jerome and Augustine, who did not regard it as hostile to Christianity. And Sidonius dedicated his translation to the Roman minister of the Visigoth king, Euric, whose court was in Bordeaux. The minister had helped the bishop get out of the prison into which the king had thrown him.[27] Before the political realignment, books sought a place in the new system. Sidonius was a contemporary of Anthemius in Rome and Proclus in Athens. But it seems to me that his interest in an important book coming out of a paganism that was barely defunct is best compared with that of Procopius of Gaza.

Pagan culture survived among the kings only at the court of Theodoric who, educated in Constantinople, surely read and wrote Greek but never learned Latin, which won him the undeserved reputation of being illiterate. His reign has remained famous because of Boethius—philosopher, engineer, poet, statesman (from about 507 until his execution in 524), and of course a Christian.

At the same court was another outstanding man of letters, descendant of a family that had dominated Bruttium for three generations—Cassiodorus, whose career began at the same time as that of Boethius and continued under Theodoric's successor until 537. After 540 the scholar Cassiodorus retired to his native province and founded on his family's estate the monastery of Vivarium, famous for its library and its copyists. Intellectual life found refuge in the abbeys and at the courts of bishops such as Isidore of Seville (ca. 570–636), the last representative of the encyclopedic Roman tradition.[28]

Pagan Becomes Peasant

In the West, a century after the definitive interdict decreed by Theodosius I and nearly a generation after the collapse of imperial power in that half of his domain, paganism, finally deserving the explanation often given today for its name, was of concern only to peasants. In Galicia during the second half of the sixth century Martin, bishop of Bracara (Braga), evangelized peasants of Suebian origin, whose kings had already been converted. He spoke about their beliefs as though they mirrored current Greco-Roman mythology, with all its scandalous legends rehashed for generations by Christian apologists. This same attitude, which was seen in connection with the statues of Menouthis, was adopted by Gregory of Tours toward the Gallic countryside.[29] Paganism was no longer worth refuting, nor even inquiring into, and for the first time a bishop referred to it "as a constituted religion."[30]

At the very end of the sixth century a series of letters by Pope Gregory the Great show him trying to convert the Barbaricini of Sardinia. Only their duke, Hospito, was a Christian. Later, Gregory discovered that the pagan peasants of that island paid the governor to be allowed to sacrifice with impunity. Even when they happened to have themselves baptized, the governor continued to demand the tax on their sacrifices![31] Gregory was above all concerned with the conversion of people outside the Empire, or those who came into it from outside, toward whom he recommended a degree of clemency at the outset.[32]

In Sicily and even in Latium, in the diocese of Terracina, peasants continued to worship idols or trees.[33] But from that time on, their religion falls out of the scope of history. We must look for its chance remains in folklore, as in Gaul where those powerful Celtic divinities, the Mothers (*Matres*) became evil spirits, the *Martes* or *Martres* who lie in wait for the late-working plowman, behind a dark mist at some corner of his field.[34] And the fairies themselves, at least to judge from their French name, *fées*, are none other than a weakened avatar of the Latin Fates, the *Fata*. The names endured, but the tradition was definitively broken.

· 10 ·

The Tenacity of the East

AMID the violent upheavals shaking the West, the paganism of intellectuals was doomed to extinction once intellectual circles became identified with clerical ones. Among the rest of the population, lacking theologians or celebrants capable of maintaining a minimum of coherency in the rituals, paganism survived merely as the dark secret of a past ever more remote under the Church triumphant.

In the East, Christian orthodoxy was no less triumphant, but the great power—Sassanid Persia followed by Islam—that bordered the Roman Empire on its eastern side could offer a haven to religious dissidents, mostly Christians. A few pagans also benefited. Within the Empire, despite natural catastrophes (earthquakes and floods) and war, a measure of stability and prosperity unknown in the West allowed fringe groups to hold out much longer. Their numbers diminished continuously—in a way that is imperceptible today—at times falling radically when they were subjected to violent repressions. Only such episodes had a chance of being remembered down to the present. It is no longer possible to write a history of the pagans after the sixth century, nor even of the persecution of paganism. One can only observe the behavior of a few social groups on the rare occasions when a chronicler, memorialist, or traveler casts a bit of light on them.

The Intolerance of the Laws

The name of one emperor remains associated with the official extirpation of paganism, Justinian (527–565), builder of Hagia Sophia and temporary restorer of the Roman Empire. Justinian, who shared power from the time his uncle Justin I ascended the throne in 518, governed alone after his uncle's death on August 1, 527. As of that year, even before his personal reign began, Justinian tightened the laws against heretics, Manichaeans, Samaritans, pagans, and the like.[1] Stakes were set up to burn Manichaeans, and the law passed against them that year contained a statement of general intolerance: "With regard to heretics, and also Hellenes who try to introduce polytheism, as well as Jews and Samaritans, we have resolved not only to restore the regulations of existing laws and to reinforce them with this present law, but also to enforce other measures which will provide those who share our shining faith with greater security, order, and honor."[2]

The prohibition against owning Christian slaves, imposed on Jews by Constantius II and his brother Constans in 339, was doubtless extended to pagans during this same period.[3] A few years later Justinian reinstated the forcible constraint in religious matters. The document published at the time is somewhat verbose but very clear. The emperor declares: "one finds persons possessed by the error of the unclean and abominable Hellenes, and performing their practices, and this arouses in God, in his love for mankind, a righteous anger." He recalls that earlier he had sought to correct them and, though with clemency, punished those who "brought sacrifices to idols in their foolish error and celebrated holidays associated with every kind of impurity." From then on he became more severe, first toward converted Hellenes relapsing into their former error, who would be sentenced to "supreme punishments," and then toward ordinary pagans:

All those who have not yet been baptized must come forward, whether they reside in the capital or in the provinces, and go to the very holy churches with their wives, their children, and their households, to be instructed in the true faith of Christians. And once thus instructed and having sincerely renounced their former error, let them be judged worthy of redemptive baptism. Should they disobey, let them know that they will be excluded from the State and will no longer have any rights of possession, neither goods nor property; stripped of everything, they will be reduced to penury, without prejudice to the appropriate punishments that will be imposed on them.

This is followed by specific regulations, for professors, peasants (if landowners, their properties will be confiscated and they will be banished), those who practice pagan cults (the death penalty), young children (to be baptized without delay), older children (to receive instruction before baptism), heads of families who receive baptism without their families (they will lose their jobs), and so on. The first of these stipulations concerns professors: "We forbid anyone stricken with the madness of the impure Hellenes to teach, so as to prevent them, under the guise of teaching those who by misfortune happen to attend their classes, from in fact corrupting the souls of those they pretend to educate. They will not receive state pensions, having no license either by Sacred Scripture or earthly law, to claim for themselves any immunity whatsoever."[4]

The word translated as "license" is *parrhesia*, which for more than a thousand years designated an essential attribute of the free man: freedom of speech. Very few ever enjoyed this freedom, and by Late Antiquity it had more than likely atrophied. The authoritarian tone that rescinds it in this document nevertheless sounds as though an era had just come to an end. The freedom of conscience instituted two centuries earlier by the edict of 313 was permanently abolished, and it is not without melancholy that one rereads its language: "It seemed to us a very good and very reasonable system to refuse to none of our subjects, whether a Christian or belonging to some other cult, the right to follow the religion that suits him best. In this way, the supreme divinity, whom each of us will forthwith venerate freely, can accord to each of us his customary favor and benevolence."[5]

From Justinian on, all pagans were condemned to civil death. The laws passed against them went as far as the privacy of the family: the son who converted was removed from the authority of his father; as for the son who remained a pagan, he was incapacitated, and the inheritance passed to relatives of the orthodox confession. In short, as Justinian said on the subject of heretics, "it is more than enough [for them] merely to be alive."[6]

The laws of 529 immediately resulted in trials of high personages in the capital, along with death penalties and a suicide, though a few acquittals. A wealthy patrician (the title conferred on former consuls or prefects; later, under Justinian, it referred more broadly to high-ranking officers), Phocas, whitewashed on that occasion, was named pretorian prefect at the time of the "Nika sedition" (January 13–18, 532), which almost cost Justinian his throne and his life, and ended in a massacre at the hippodrome leaving somewhere between 30,000 to 50,000 dead. Phocas then presided over the initial construction of Hagia Sophia.[7] But in October he was removed from a post that Justinian had merely given him in an attempt, which proved useless, to placate the populace. New investigations were undertaken in 545 by a Monophysite monk, John of Ephesus, a native of Amida (Diyarbakir), whom we come across in other episodes of the persecution of pagans. "Illustrious and noble men, along with a host of grammarians [professors of literature], sophists, scholastics [lawyers], and doctors" were subjected to torture and confis-cation of property. Fearing another trial, Phocas this time took poison. "When the emperor found out, he ordered, and rightfully, that [Phocas] be buried like a donkey."[8] In Constan-tinople, a Christian city of long standing, paganism seems to have survived only among the aristocracy—those primarily affected by the dictatorial emperor's persecution of paganism.

Justinian and the School of Athens

A very famous episode from the period 529–532—the closing of the Neoplatonist school of Athens—must be placed within the general framework of the measures taken at the begin-ning of Justinian's reign in order to be understood. To do otherwise would minimize its significance.[9]

Intellectual paganism had remained alive in Athens during the first quarter of the sixth century, though not without risk. It seems to have escaped the major crises that threatened it in Alexandria and Beirut, and that offered the Christians of those cities a pretext for devastating attacks on the decaying cults. As we have seen in the case of Proclus, the situation in Athens was unique: the school of philosophy, the Academy, was well endowed, thanks to funds provided at the begin-ning of the fifth century by Plutarch and later by other do-nors.[10] The institution did not depend solely on fees paid by its pupils. The situation was very different when Libanius came there to study, around 336, or when Synesius visited Athens, probably around the end of the fourth century and found "nothing impressive about Athens any longer except the names of famous sites. Like the victim at the end of a sac-rifice, only its skin remains to identify what it used to be."[11]

Proclus and Damascius represent subsequent renewals. During the fifth century the fortunes of the school depended exclusively on the quality of its professors and on the inevitable rivalries that divided them. A fragment by Damascius may allude to this: "Because of the sedition [or discord], Marinus left Athens for Epidaurus, suspecting plots that included one on his own life." [12] Does this have to do with Christian riots that forced Marinus to seek refuge in Epidaurus for a while—or merely discord among philosophers? The latter would better explain why Marinus seems to be the only one threatened by intrigues, from which he readily escaped merely by crossing the Saronic Gulf.

Athens was a small town where teaching had always been a distinguished career and a source of pride. It was unlike Alexandria or Beirut, having neither their power of Christian religious authority nor their host of believers. The Academy, outstanding under Proclus or Isidorus, declined under Hegias, but regained its prestige under Damascius, who was the director when Justinian closed it in 529. At the time it was abolished, it was neither in decline nor in crisis. Under Anastasius (491–518), the poet Christodorus of Coptos wrote a book "on the listeners of the great Proclus," as well as descriptions of works of art and accounts of the traditions of great cities. Proclus' pupils cut a rather funny picture as monuments of classical culture. At the same time John of Lydia, a high official curious about ancient history, took pride in declaring that he had acquired a smattering of Aristotle and Plato through contact with a pupil of Proclus who lived in the capital. [13]

The meaning of Justinian's dramatic gesture has been widely discussed. Alan Cameron interprets it as restrictive. In 529 Justinian prohibited pagans from teaching. [14] The measure, Cameron believes, applied only to philosophy, and only to Athens. Other schools—of law in Beirut, rhetoric in Gaza, and philosophy in Alexandria—continued to function. The Academy appeared to be "subversive." Furthermore, its wealth was of a magnitude to whet the appetite of the tax collectors. In Alexandria, on the other hand, pagans such as

Ammonius and Olympiodorus after him continued to teach and publish until 565, perhaps because of the mysterious "agreement" between Ammonius and the patriarch related by Damascius (who was less fortunate with the authorities than his rival), but more likely because in Alexandria they principally studied Aristotle, who antagonized Christians less than Plato. In Alexandria at the beginning of the seventh century a Christian professor, Stephanus, taught in his courses the eternity of the world according to Aristotle, without trying to refute the master or to reconcile his views with Christianity.[15] In the fifteenth century when Sultan Mehmet II, intellectually more captivating than the somber Justinian, conquered Constantinople, the Aristotelians displayed the same tendency to adapt to a new power, whereas the Platonists emigrated to Italy.

The Academy's endowment was confiscated by the emperor toward the end of 531 or the beginning of 532.[16] The philosophers of Athens then sought refuge in Mesopotamia among the Persians. This is surely one of the most fabulous episodes of the period: the worshipers of the Sun marching East, taking with them the treasures of Hellenic wisdom. According to Agathias, they were seven, like the planets they worshiped and the sages of ancient Greece. These facile symbols would not, by themselves, make the episode any less historical. Chosroes, the young sovereign on the throne of the Sassanid empire, invited them to his court; he wanted scholars around him. When he failed to hold the philosophers, he succeeded in retaining an Aristotelian doctor, Uranius, about whom the historian Agathias, born in 532, paints the unflattering portrait of a charlatan, a great speechmaker when drunk, carrying on discussions with the Zoroastrian priests of Persia, the *magi*, about the eternity of the world.[17] The mediocrity of Uranius highlights the talent of those who preceded him—the flower of contemporary Greek philosophy.

What could they have been seeking in the court of Chosroes? They might have been prompted by intellectual curiosity, by the desire to find an alternative to Christianity. We may suppose that this impulse was analogous to the one that led the last pagans to foreign gods. However, although Zoroastrianism does not exclude polytheism, Chosroes was not really a pagan. According to Agathias, the philosophers imagined the Persians as honest and sincere, in short, virtuous. This idealized and rather naive image apparently was inspired by the works of Herodotus and Xenophon, written a thousand years earlier. They would have sung a different tune very quickly, when confronted by a harsher, more hierarchical, and less hellenized society than the one they expected to find. And they would have shrunk from the task of teaching their beloved doctrines to Persian courtiers, little inclined to asceticism, through the raucous sounds and inevitable inexactitude of Pahlavi interpreters.

Greeks were shocked by Zoroastrian religious customs, such as leaving the dead in special places for dogs and vultures to pick the bones clean, so as to prevent the earth from coming into contact with corpses. Agathias quotes an epigram, placed in the mouth of a Zoroastrian ghost whose corpse the philosophers tried to bury: "Do not bury one who should not be buried, leave him as prey for dogs; the Earth, universal mother, does not receive a man who soils his mother."

These lines underscore the Zoroastrians' obsession with preventing the earth from being sullied, and on the endogamous tendencies of Persian society that even sanctioned the marriage of mother and son—what could be more Oedipal! The epigram, which seems to have been written ("revealed in a dream") by a member of the expedition on their return trip, undoubtedly expresses their overall disenchantment. But it lacks originality, and any idiosyncratic particular: the classical tradition had long been scandalized by the matrimonial customs of the Persians.[18] The general imprecision and purely rhetorical character of the expedition's account in Agathias has led Michel Tardieu to deny all historicity to the story, which would have been forged to strengthen the claims of Simplicius and his followers to live in Carrhae.

According to Agathias' narrative, Chosroes' guests left after spending a few months at his court, but without having quarreled. The fiction lent credence to the pretense that the peace concluded in 532 between the Persian king and Justinian guaranteed the safety of their persons and their eventual return home to live "as they chose."[19] Damascius apparently retired to his native province of Syria (he was from Damascus). In Emesa [Homs, 105 miles north of Damascus] an epitaph for a female slave has been found dated 538; it is also recorded in *The Palatine Anthology* where it is attributed to Damascius:

> I, Zosimus, who until now was a slave only in body,
> Now have I obtained freedom for my body as well.[20]

Damascius' disciples, especially Simplicius, did not return to Athens, although they continued to write. Tardieu has shown that Simplicius settled in Carrhae (Harran), within Roman territory but beyond the Euphrates, near the Persian border, and there established a Neoplatonist school. It remained active for nearly five centuries in a milieu that was and continued to be hospitable. As a matter of fact, although Carrhae—Abraham's stopover on his way to Canaan, and the land of Laban where Jacob met Rachel near the famous well— attracted Christian pilgrims and monks, the population had remained pagan. In the spring of 384, Lady Egeria, who had come from Galicia, made a long detour on her way to Jerusalem in order to stop in Harran. She chanced to arrive during the feast day of a local saint, Helpidius, and was able to meet with the monks of Mesopotamia, "but when night fell they returned to the desert, each to his own hermitage. In the city, outside of a small number of priests and the holy monks who lived there, I did not find a single Christian, but there were pagans everywhere."[21]

After the campaign of 540, during which Chosroes invaded Syria, sacking, depopulating, and partially destroying Antioch, the conqueror exempted Carrhae from paying a tribute because "a majority" of its population was faithful "to the ancient religion."[22] Manichaeans had also taken refuge there. During the truces between Romans and Sassanians, if a clause granted some freedom of conscience, it was not to benefit a handful of vagrant philosophers. It was to guarantee border inhabitants that they would not suffer too much at the hands of their temporary master.

In the ninth century Tabit ben Qurra, the Harranian founder of the School of Baghdad, declared that his birthplace had "never been sullied by the error of Nazareth."[23] Shortly before 946, the Arab traveler al Masudi, when visiting Harran, saw "on the door knocker of the meeting place of the Sabians, an inscription in Syriac characters, taken from Plato. It was explained to me by Malik ben Uqbun and other people of the same sect: 'He who knows his nature becomes god.'"

Tardieu recognized this as a quotation from the *First Alcibiades* (133 c), which Platonists considered the very gateway to their master's doctrine.[24] The fundamental affirmation at the core of the teaching of these "Sabians"—there is "a cause in the world that has never ceased: a monad, not a multiple, which is affected by none of the attributes whatever of the things caused"—reflects the theories of Proclus and extends the metaphysics of the *Parmenides* on the subject of the One and the many, the holy of holies of late Platonism.[25] Throughout the centuries the Aramaicized heirs of Plato, Plotinus, Porphyry, and Proclus kept their rituals, prayers, fasts, sacrifices (especially of cocks, the solar animal, an offering made by Socrates as his final sacrifice), and, within the school, use of the old Attic calendar which was both solar and lunar.[26] They claimed the name of pagans, but their meeting place was separate from the pagan temples of the city, only one of which was still functioning in the tenth century. It was through the intermediary of the school of Harran that Greek philosophy reached Baghdad, whence it returned to the West, translated into Arabic, via Muslim Andalusia. As for the school of Harran, it disappeared in the eleventh century during the unrest caused by the arrival of the Seljuk Turks in Iraq.[27]

Justinian's closure of the school at Athens left an echo on the Roman side, in the writings of John Malalas, a historian from Antioch, and Agathias of Myrina, a pious Christian who devoted several pages of his *Histories* to it.[28] However, this does not quite mark the end of philosophy outside of Alexandria and Carrhae. As late as the reign of Heraclius (610–641), the emperor brought the Neoplatonist Stephanus from Alexandria to Constantinople in order to offer him a chair of philosophy.[29] But inside the Byzantine Empire, since Justinian's edicts, philosophy had lost its radiance.

The Last Refuges of Paganism

On occasion, an archaeological find discloses a halt in the general retreat of paganism. In 515 at Zoara, an Arabian locality just south of the Dead Sea, Theandrites, a god venerated by Proclus and Isidorus, was replaced by Saint George. Stones bearing ex-votos to the fallen god were used again in the new masonry, and an inscription dated March 22, 515, lyrically evokes the transformation of the temple into a church: "God has his dwelling where there was once a hostel of demons; redeeming light now shines where once darkness spread its veil; where once sacrifices were made to idols, angels now dance."[30]

Occasionally we also see a kind of coexistence between the two cults, as when Christians were in a small minority or when the pagan god was protected by the worship of powerful neighbors outside imperial authority. We have the example of the bishop of Harran, who must have felt somewhat lonely in his city. In Baalbek a church had been standing in the courtyard of the colossal temple of Jupiter Heliopolitan ever since the reign of Theodosius I, at the end of the fourth century. Nonetheless, "no one had been able to discredit" the ancient Baal of the Bekaa Valley by 555, the year lightning severely damaged the pagan ruins. "This temple, above all because of its splendor,. kept the pagans in their error," Bishop John of Ephesus acknowledged at the time.[31]

On the island of Philae in Egypt the presence of Christian churches did not prevent the temple of Isis from remaining in use. Between 449 and 468, the wall that protected the island was restored by the military governor of the Theban border with the bishop's help in collecting and distributing funds. As Etienne Bernand, the last editor of the inscription that disclosed this construction, remarked, "Bishop Daniel was concerned with fortifying the island, not with exorcising the temple of Isis." Also found were a number of dedications dating from the same years, made by a priestly family that served the temple, perhaps on behalf of the fearsome Blemyes. Under a peace treaty concluded with the Romans in 451–452, this tribe came every year from the Sudan to fetch the statue of Isis. They carried it to their territory where she made prophecies for them, and then returned it to her temple, until the following year. In 537 Narses, duke of the Thebaid, a Persian-Armenian general won over to Rome, permanently closed the temple. The statues (Isis, Osiris, and "Priapus," which is probably Min) were sent to Byzantium and the priests were jailed.[32]

Augila (Awjidah) in Cyrenaica, far to the west of Siwa, seems to have maintained a sanctuary to "Ammon and Alexander the Great" under Justinian, who prided himself on suppressing the cult, building a church in its stead and installing a bishop in that remote oasis. We may well wonder today what gods those Saharan Berbers worshiped, 400 kilometers south of Cyrene, a four days' march from Boreion, a small Jewish settlement on the shore of the Syrte, that the evangelical emperor also Christianized during the same campaign. Did Alexander the Great really inspire their adoration? Justinian's act established him as a missionary whose successes went all the way to the ends of the inhabited earth, the *oikoumene*; his prestige only stood to gain from his encounter with the shade of the great conqueror.[33]

John the Inquisitor

On the basis of this evidence, we might get the impression that under Justinian paganism was finally eradicated. It does not seem to have survived even in the desert outposts to which it was ultimately relegated. It was pushed to the edge of the Empire and the fringe of society with the Platonists of Harran. And yet, the episodes that are vividly related in enormous detail by John of Ephesus, a monk then bishop, bring us back to the heart of the Empire and within close range of the emperor. In 542 John of Ephesus became the chargé d'affaires for pagans, *super paganos*, in Asia (meaning the western part of Asia Minor): Caria, Phrygia, and Lydia. Shortly thereafter, in 545–546, he evangelized the mountainous area around Tralles in Asia Minor, in the lower valley of the Meander, in the region of Ephesus, near the Aegean coast. Tralles was at that time a flourishing city, according to Agathias. Christodorus of Coptus wrote a poem about its traditions, and it was the birthplace of Anthemius, one of the architects of Hagia Sophia.[34]

John cleansed the countryside around a large city, a region where the mountains stand in striking contrast to the flatness of the surrounding landscape. The mountains and plain are completely different—in topography, resources, climate, and even population. An ethnographic study made by Altan Gökalp in the region of Aydın (the Turkish name for Tralles) has shown how, in a predominantly Sunni population, these mountains have provided a refuge for a solitary group of Shiite "Red Hats" resettled in hilltop villages where approaching strangers can be seen from a great distance.[35]

The inquisitor himself described his campaign. He built twenty-four churches and four monasteries and destroyed "a house of idols" where the pagans held annual celebrations with their priests. John became bishop of Ephesus in 558 and in 562 unleashed new persecutions.[36] Even though his fidelity to Monophysitism had previously forced him into secrecy and imprisonment, he had the support not only of the empress Theodora (who died in 548), herself a cobeliever, but also of Justinian, who paid for the expenses and robes of the baptisms John administered and contributed one-third of gold coin (*aureus*) given to each of the new Christians. They then helped to destroy the temples, overturn the idols, break the altars, and "cut down the many trees they used to worship."

The great persecution, for us the final episode (there must have been numerous lesser ones that did not find their John of Ephesus to chronicle them), took place during the second year of the reign of Justinian's successor, Tiberius (from 580 on). Tiberius, having sent a general to repress an uprising of Jews and Samaritans, ordered him to take care of the pagans in Heliopolis (Baalbek) along the way. The Bekaa Valley was subjected to a reign of terror: "He arrested many of them . . . humiliated them, crucified them, and killed them." Under torture, his victims denounced their coreligionists, who were "in most of the cities of the East and particularly in Antioch." They included Anatolius, the governor of the province, who was planning to take part in a secret ceremony to honor Zeus at the home of a pagan priest in Edessa. When the police surrounded the house, the priest committed suicide with a razor. The faithful, seeing the police arrive, stayed away, but their names were revealed by the priests' servants, an old invalid and his aged wife, who were arrested beside their master's body and cult objects. Anatolius, hoping to establish an alibi, rode off in travel clothes to the bishop's house in the middle of the night, pretending that he wanted to discuss a question of Scripture with him. He was arrested as he left the bishopric.

The case was immediately heard by the judges of Antioch. Denunciations followed in torrents. The patriarch of Antioch and a monk who had since become the bishop of Alexandria were implicated in a case of human sacrifice in Daphne. Following this, the informer, who was Anatolius' secretary, was found dead in his prison cell, presumably killed to prevent him from revealing any more information. "For the honor of Christianity" the authorities decided to stop harassing the bishops. On the other side, during a house search, Anatolius fell victim to what seemed to be a divine judgment: an icon of Christ that he had hung in his house to testify to his faith turned its face toward the wall three times. After careful examination, it was discovered that the icon concealed an image of Apollo in such a way as to prevent detection. That was the end of Anatolius, who was taken to Constantinople with the other defendants. The trial took place behind closed doors.

But those closed doors aroused suspicion among the people. Were the judges corruptible? Would they be tolerant toward paganism? The city had been in an uproar ever since the events in Antioch. This time riots took place all along the city's central artery (the *Mese*, presently *Divan yolu*), with their concomitant looting and fires. The rioters threatened the bishop and invaded the courtroom. Their furor was at its peak when they broke open the cabinet containing the bail warrants: it was filled with gold. Two unfortunate defendants, a man and a woman, who probably had been the only ones not to pay bail, were caught, dragged to the port, and put aboard a boat. The mob told the executioner to burn them alive. When he refused, the rioters threw him on the boat with the two suspected pagans and set fire to it. The executioner managed to save himself; the other two perished by fire and by water.

The mob then continued on to the prisons. "The pagans were let go, why should Christians be held?" So the prisons were emptied of some good Christians, albeit felons. The prefect of the Praetorium managed to save his palace from being looted by convincing the rioters that he was on their side. He was obliged to accompany them to the emperor, leaving behind his insignia of office. At the imperial palace words were exchanged "that could not be put in writing." Tiberius placated the rioters by promising to give them what they wanted. He quickly organized games, meanwhile preparing to have troops massacre his subjects in case the uprising started again, which it did not. The inquest was resumed under the direction of a more zealous prefect. Since culprits were needed for the previous uprisings, a few well-placed tortures revealed that the true criminals were—rather surprisingly for us, if not to a Byzantine mind—the Jews, the Samaritans, and the Montanists. They crucified some, whipped others, and still others were sent into a variety of exiles. As for those Christians whose part was investigated, their punishment was a charade: lash marks were simulated on their backs with leeches and red paint, and they were paraded around the city on muleback. Then "the Christians were pardoned. But the Jews who were found were arrested and brought to trial."

After such preliminaries the sentences of those accused during the great trial could be nothing but severe. Anatolius was not only condemned to death, he was tortured, clawed by wild animals, and finally crucified. The cadavers of the condemned were "treated like donkey carcasses," dragged through the streets and thrown outside the walls on public trash heaps. The inquisitions continued after the death of Tiberius (582), under his successor, Maurice, the victims thrown to wild beasts and then burned. Unhappy they who observed a few rituals from the ancient religion after they were baptized! All of this seems to herald the torments inflicted, much later and with greater perseverance, on the Marranos of Catholic Spain. "And that is why every day more are denounced and they receive the just desserts of their actions, in this world and in the next," John of Ephesus complacently concludes.[37] His extraordinary account was written while the witch hunt was still going on.

I am often tempted when reading him to superimpose on his text images of other riots in Istanbul: Janissaries demanding of the sultan the head of some grand vizier, or, more recently, the riots against Armenians at the end of the nineteenth century, or against the Greeks in 1954. But it would be facile and erroneous to suggest that in Istanbul, as in Alexandria at the time of the lynching of Hypatia, there is a geographic or "climatic" determinism at work. Religious fanaticism owes nothing to latitude or ethnic origin, nor even much to the religion in whose name it is practiced. It would be more appropriate to say that the Christian mob in Byzantium was irritated by the aristocratic character of paganism, which they saw as collusion between powers beyond their understanding. However intolerable they found this, the people had nothing better to propose, so the movement was in no way revolutionary and ran itself dry in pogroms, followed by the bloody spectacles of executions. The paganism of high officials did indeed have its popular supporters, but in provinces removed from the central power, such as the isolated Bekaa, and in Osrhoene, where Edessa was assuredly a Christian city, though close to Harran and its unrepentant pagans.

Evidently there were other pockets of paganism and armed missionaries from Byzantium ventured out into some of them very late. The Laconians, isolated on the arid rocky peninsula of Mani, but protected by that very geography and prosperous because of their excellent olives, were not converted until the reign of Basil I in the ninth century. It is explicitly said by our source that these were not Slavs, as was so often the case in the Peloponnesus at the time, but descendants of the ancient population of the region.[38] We probably will never know the nature of their religion. With them, in this impoverished center of Greece, my chronicle of dogged rural paganism ends.

Epilogue

$\mathcal{A}$ND yet, the tracks of the last pagans are not completely lost in the sands of folklore, nor do they entirely disappear behind the screen of Islam. Rather, they resurface at the end of the fifteenth century, three hundred years after the school of Harran had been swept away. A talented young Greek, who had become suspect to the church authorities of his country—by then reduced to one city, Constantinople—left to study for a time among the people across the way, the Ottoman Turks. He did not have far to go: whether to Edirne or to Bursa, it was at most a journey of a few days that brought him to a refined and multilingual court. There he made the acquaintance of a Jew, Elissaios,

attached to Averroes and to other Persian and Arab commentators of Aristotle whom the Jews had translated into their own language. As for Moses and what the Jews believe and practice through his intermediary, that did not concern him at all. It was that man who taught him the doctrines of Zoroaster and others. Through this man, a Jew in appearance but more accurately a pagan, whom he not only long regarded as his teacher, but whom he served as needed and who supported him, for this man, Elissaios by name, was one of the most powerful people at the court of those barbarians, through this man, then, he succeeded in becoming who he was.[1]

Who was the young Greek? The philosopher Georgius Gemistus, called Plethon. He later returned to Constantinople, but his method of explicating Aristotle displeased the religious authorities, and so he settled in Mistra, in the southern part of the Peloponnesus, near Mani, which was then the capital of a Byzantine principality. He died there in 1452, one year before Mehmet II conquered Constantinople.

Plethon traveled only once to the West, accompanying the Greek delegation to the Council of Florence (1438–1439). The group desperately sought unification with Rome in the vain hope that the termination of the schism would protect the last Byzantines from the crushing superiority of the Turks. But Plethon's ideas traveled throughout Renaissance Europe— thanks to his illustrious disciples, the Greek John Bessarion, who ended up as a cardinal of the Roman church, and the Florentine Marsilio Ficino—and had an extraordinary effect.[2] By whatever means, the torch was passed during the three centuries that separated the closing of the school of Harran and Plethon's apprenticeship with Elissaios. The philosophical paganism of Late Antiquity made its contribution to the birth of the world in which we still live.

Notes · Index

NOTES

Introduction

1. Averil Cameron and J. Herrin, eds., *Constantinople in the Early Eighth Century: The Parastaseis Syntomoi Chronikai* (Leiden, 1984); Cyril Mango, "Antique Statuary and the Byzantine Beholder," *Dumbarton Oaks Papers* 17 (1963): 53–75.
2. Louis Robert, *Hellenica* IV (1948): 108.
3. Commentary and examples ibid., pp. 5–34.
4. Ibid., p. 109.

1. What Is a Pagan?

1. *Contra,* J. Zeiller, *Paganus. Etude de terminologie historique* (Paris and Fribourg, 1917).
2. A. H. M. Jones, "The Social Background of the Struggle between Paganism and Christianity," in A. Momigliano, ed., *The Conflict between Paganism and Christianity in the Fourth Century* (Oxford, 1963), p. 17.
3. Theodore Zahn, "Paganus," *Neue Kirchl. Zeitschr.*, 1899, pp. 18–44; opposing arguments by Zeiller, *Paganus,* pp. 43–58.
4. For Persius, I return to Néméthy's interpretation in his edition of the *Satires* (Budapest, 1903), p. 50, against Zeiller, *Paganus,* p. 27. For the Roman epitaph (2nd century A.D.?), see ibid., p. 11.
5. I. Gothofredus (Jacques Godefroy), *De statu paganorum sub christianis imperatoribus, seu commentarium ad titulum X, De paganis, libri XVI Codicis Theodosiani* (1616), p. 19: *paganos . . . dictos . . . pro pagorum diversitate sacris inter se diversos.*
6. Ibn Arabi, quoted by M. Chodkiewicz, *Le sceau des saints. Prophétie et sainteté dans la doctrine d'Ibn Arabi* (Paris, 1986), p. 18.
7. Alan Cameron, "The Last Days of the Academy at Athens," *Proc. Cambridge Philological Soc.*, 1969, pp. 7–29; p. 9, quoting A. H. M. Jones.
8. Similarly, the sophisticated organization of imperial power, its

administration and its army, does not require description here. It was however necessary to use such terms as "Augustus," "Caesar," and "pretorian prefect"; in the religious domain "Arian," and "Monophysite"; and in architecture "basilica."

9. For the *Life of Constantine*, see Chapter 3, note 5. For the *Life of Porphyry*, see Chapter 6, note 11. Byzantine historians constantly imitate "classical" writers such as Thucydides and Herodotus; yet this in no way vitiates their accuracy. In the face of what may at first appear to be a literary commonplace, a *topos*, one must wonder whether it is not reality that is repeating itself. For example, the historical account, however fanciful, of a king who says he will give his daughter to a foreign sovereign and gives him instead a slave in disguise; discovery of the truth leads to a war. This example and references can be found in H. Hunger, *Die hochsprachliche profane Literatur der Byzantiner* (Munich, 1978), I, 284.

2. An Empire in Search of Religion

1. L. Robert, "Une vision de Perpétue martyre à Carthage en 203," *Comptes rendus Acad. Inscr.*, 1982, pp. 228–276, esp. 253–266 (Perpetua sees Christ in a dream as an agonothete); on Pionios, *id.*, *Op. min. sel.* (1960), p. 835, n. 1. For a general introduction to the period, see Peter Brown, *The Making of Late Antiquity* (Cambridge, Mass., 1978); and R. L. Fox, *Pagans and Christians in the Mediterranean World from the Second Century A.D. to the Conversion of Constantine* (New York, 1987), on which see the review by G. Fowden, *Jour. Rom. St.*, 1988, pp. 173–182.

2. W. H. C. Frend, *The Rise of Christianity* (London, 1984), pp. 368 ff.; *Martyrdom and Persecution in the Early Church. A Study of a Conflict from the Maccabees to Donatus* (Oxford, 1965), p. 446, referring to E. Venables, in the *Dict. of Christ. Biogr.*, I, 111.

3. L. Duchesne, "Le concile d'Elvire et les flamines chrétiens," *Mélanges Renier* (Paris, 1887), pp. 159–174 (council before 303); V. C. de Clercq, *Ossius of Cordova. A Contribution to the History of the Constantinian Period* (Washington, D.C., 1954), pp. 87–103 (council about 300); Frend, *Martyrdom*, pp. 447–448 (council in 309, after H. Grégoire); T. D. Barnes, *Constantine and Eusebius* (Cambridge, Mass., 1981), p. 314, n. 108 (before 303). In my opinion, the main argument in favor of a date before the persecutions is the lack of any allusions to apostasy through fear of civil authorities in the conciliary dispositions; in favor of a later date is the great similarity between the con-

cerns of the Elvira bishops and those of the Arles council (314).

4. The *PLRE* I distinguishes between the director of the purple dye factories and the martyr, mistakenly in my view; cf. Frend, *Martyrdom*, pp. 485 ff., after Lactantius, *De mort. persecut.*, 15, and Eusebius, *Hist. Eccles.*, VIII, 1, 3.

5. Momigliano, introduction to *Conflict between Paganism and Christianity*, p. 6. The contrast between pagans and Christians is clearly demonstrated by Fox, *Pagans and Christians*, pp. 13–16, who contrasts two third-century "careers," that of an Athenian aristocrat and man of letters, T. Flavius Glaucus, and that of a rhetor who became bishop of Carthage, Cyprian.

6. Origen, *Contra Celsus*, I, 43, III, 9–10; cited by Frend, *Martyrdom*, p. 403; my exposition essentially follows this book, pp. 403–569.

7. Roger Bagnall, "Religious Conversion and Onomastic Change in Early Byzantine Egypt," *Bull. of the Amer. Soc. of Papyrol.*, 1983, pp. 105–129, and "Conversion and Onomastics: A Reply," *Zeitschr. für Pap. und Epigr.* 69 (1984): 243–250.

8. On the controversial date of that rescript, see L. D. Bruce, "Diocletian, the Proconsul Julianus and the Manichaeans," *Studies in Latin Literature and Roman History* (Brussels, 1983), III, 336–347, and reviews by Michel Tardieu in *Etudes manichéennes. Bibliographie critique, 1977–1986*, Abstracta Iranica series, no. 4, 1988, esp. IV, 379; V, 488; VI, 408; C, 23; C, 53.

9. Barnes, *Constantine and Eusebius*, p. 21.

10. Eusebius, *Hist. Eccles.*, VIII, 6, 8; see also, for Syria, Libanius, I (*Autobiography*), 3; XI (*Antiochicus*), 158–162; XIX, 45–46; XX, 18–20.

11. I take the comparison from A. K. Bowman, *Egypt after the Pharaohs, 332 B.C.–A.D. 642* (Berkeley, 1986), pp. 191–192. *P. Oxy.* 2601 is mentioned also by Barnes, *Constantine and Eusebius*, p. 296, n. 83. For governors in North Africa, see ibid., p. 295, n. 57.

12. Frend, *Martyrdom*, pp. 498, 529, after Eusebius, *Mart. Pal.*, 3, 1. See also ibid., 13, 4, and *Hist. Eccles.*, VIII, 13, 5.

13. Eusebius, *Hist. Eccles.*, IX, 2, 3, 7; Lactantius, *De mortibus persecut.*, 36, 3; for Lycia and Pamphylia, see inscription from Arycanda in *TAM*, II, 3, 785; cf. F. Millar, *The Emperor in the Roman World* (London, 1977), pp. 445 ff.; for Colbasa, see St. Mitchell, "Maximinus and the Christians in A.D. 312: A New Latin Inscription," *Jour. Rom. St.* 78 (1988): 105–124 (p. 123 for projected abolition of the poll tax).

14. Frend, *Martyrdom*, pp. 506, 531.

15. B. Levick, *Journal of Hellenic Studies*, 1971, pp. 80–84.

16. Gaston Boissier, *La fin du paganisme. Etude sur les dernières luttes religieuses en occident au quatrième siècle* (Paris, 1891), I, appendix, "Les persécutions," pp. 399–459.

17. Eusebius, *Life of Constantine*, III, 15; cited by Boissier, *Fin du paganisme*, I, 68.

3. Constantine's Christian Empire

1. *Paneg. Const.* 6 (7), 3–7, in *Panégyriques latins*, ed. E. Galletier (Paris, 1952), vol. 2. For the number of crowns (four?), see the discussion in Barnes, *Constantine and Eusebius*, p. 36 and n. 71.

2. Time and place of composition after J. L. Creed, Introduction to his edition of *De mortibus persecut.* (Oxford, 1984), pp. xxvii, xxxiii ff., xlv.

3. Lactantius, *De mortibus persecut.*, 44, 8.

4. Eusebius, *Life of Constantine*, I, 28. We are informed at para. 26 that Constantine has decided to march on Rome. The emperor holds Italy only at the end of para. 37, after he has "bound himself to God's alliance." Relations between Constantine and his panegyrist Eusebius were not as close as has been assumed by modern scholars who have trusted Eusebius' words. See Barnes, *Constantine and Eusebius*, pp. 267–268.

5. The authenticity of the *Life of Constantine* should no longer be questioned; see, for example, L. Tartaglia, *Sulla vita di Costantino*, trans. and commentary (Naples, 1984), pp. 13–17. Nevertheless, the problem of interpretation remains. The first two books are written like a traditional panegyric; books III and IV have the more historical and documented character of a Life (Averil Cameron, "La *Vita Constantini* d'Eusèbe: technique littéraire," lecture delivered at the Collège de France, Paris, Dec. 3, 1987). For the daily vision as a solar halo, see, among others, Barnes, *Constantine and Eusebius*, p. 43 and n. 148.

6. Lactantius, *De mortibus persecut.*, 48 (Latin text); Eusebius, *Hist. Eccles.*, X, 5, 4–8 (Greek text).

7. M. R. Alföldi, "Die Sol Comes-Münze vom Jahre 325. Neues zur Bekehrung Constantins," *Festschrift Th. Klauser* (Münster, 1964), pp. 10 ff.; *contra*, see L. De Giovanni, *Costantino e il mondo pagano* (Naples, 1977), pp. 105 ff.

8. R. Krautheimer, *Three Christian Capitals, Topography and Politics* (Berkeley and Los Angeles, 1983), pp. 35–40.

9. C. Pietri, "Le temps de la semaine à Rome et dans l'Italie chrétienne (IV–VIs)," *Le temps chrétien de la fin de l'Antiquité au Moyen Age, IIIe–XIIIe siècles* (Paris, 1984), pp. 63–97.

10. Libanius, *Orat.* 30, *Pro temp.*, 5. G. Dagron, *Naissance d'une capitale. Constantinople et ses institutions de 330 à 451* (Paris, 1974), pp. 388–400.

11. Cyril Mango, *Le développement urbain de Constantinople,* (Paris, 1985), pp. 25, 30.

12. John the Lydian, *Months,* IV, 2, p. 65, 2–66, l Wünsch; cited by Franz-Josef Dölger, *Sol Salutis. Gebet und Gesang im christlichen Altertum* (Münster, 1925), p. 69. On Sopater, see Millar, *Emperor,* pp. 99–100. Surprising as it may seem at first glance, such behavior should not be disregarded as fictitious. See Dölger, *Sol Salutis,* and Dagron, *Naissance d'une capitale,* p. 373.

13. Zosimus, II, 31; see Apoll. Rh., I, 1117 ff. (Argonauts to Cyzicus); Hesychios of Miletus, *Orig. Const.,* 15, and W. Amelung, "Kybele-Orans," *Röm. Mitteil.,* 1899, p. 8–12. See also Dagron, *Naissance d'une capitale,* pp. 373–374.

14. Contrary to what Krautheimer thinks; see *Three Christian Capitals,* p. 61.

15. See L. Cracco Ruggini, *Roma Costantinopoli Mosca* (Naples, 1983), pp. 241–251.

16. Mango, "Antique Statuary and the Byzantine Beholder," esp. p. 56.

17. Cod. Theod., IX, 16, 1 and 2, laws of 319 and 320; see F. Martroye, *Bull. Soc. nat. Ant. Fr.,* 1915, pp. 280–292.

18. Cod. Theod., IX, 16, 3, law promulgated in 319.

19. Ibid., XVI, 10, 1 in 320, law promulgated after lightning hit the Coliseum in Rome.

20. J. Maurice, "La terreur de la magie au IVe siècle," *Revue hist. du droit fr. et étr.,* 1927, pp. 108–120, esp. 109.

21. Inscription from Orcistus: *CIL,* III, suppl. I. 7000 = Dessau, III, 6091. In the request addressed to Constantine and to his sons, the Caesars Crispus (murdered by order of his father in 326), Constantine, and Constantius (promoted to the rank of Caesar on Nov. 8, 324), Orcistus requested that it be granted the status of a city immediately after Licinius' fall. The imperial offices did not deliver their response, it appears, until 329 or 330 for the first rescript, and on June 30, 331, for the second. See the comprehensive study by A. Chastagnol, "L'inscription chrétienne d'Orcistus," *Mél. éc. fr. de Rome, Ant.,* 1981, I, 381–416. Chastagnol assumes that Orcistus is the

small, solely Christian town that was surrounded and burned, with all its inhabitants, by Diocletian's troops in 304 or 305, which Eusebius leaves unnamed (*Hist. Eccl.*, VIII, 11, 1; cf. Lactantius, *Div. Inst.*, V, 11, 10). Orcistus would have lost its independence only after that disaster. This remains hypothetical. For the inscription from Nakoleia for Julian, see *CIL*, III, 350. See W. Ruge, *Real-Enc.*, under Nakoleia (1935), col. 1602, and Orcistus (1939), col. 1092 f.; Millar, *Emperor in the Roman World*, pp. 131, 410, 438, also cites the example of Maiouma, the Christian port of pagan Gaza that obtained independence from its metropolis and the name of Constantia.

22. *CIL*, XI, 2, 5265 = Dessau 705; J. Gascou, *Mél. Ec. fr. Rome*, 1967, 609; Millar, *Emperor in the Roman World*, p. 453. In Rome: compare Zosimus, II, 29, 5, and Libanius, *Orat.* 30, *Pro temp.*, 33.

23. Cod. Theod., XVI, 2, 5.

24. Genesis, 12, 6f. and 18, 1–15; Eusebius, *Life of Constantine*, II, 51–53; between 326 and 330. Sozomen, *Hist. Eccl.*, II, 4, 1–6, provides a vivid description of the large fair and religious festivals at Mambre, on which, see M. Tardieu, *Foires des Arabes* (forthcoming).

25. Eusebius, *Life of Constantine*, III, 55.

26. Ibid., IV, 25; cf. Libanius, *Orat.* 30, 35, and on the clergy, Greg. Naz., *Orat.* 5, 32 (PG 35, 705b) and *Nemes.*, 267 f (PG 37, 1572).

27. See L. De Giovanni, *Costantino*, pp. 99 ff.

28. Ammianus, XVIII, 4, 5, and J. B. Segal, *Edessa, "The Blessed City"* (Oxford, 1970), pp. 56, 70.

29. See Zosimus, II, 42, 1, with commentary by F. Paschoud; E. Stein and J. R. Palanque, *Histoire de Bas-Empire* (Paris, 1949, I, 133 ff.).

30. Eusebius, *Life of Constantine*, III, 56; the date according to Sozomen, *Hist. Eccl.*, II, 4, 5, (57 Bidez); Julian's order, according to Zonaras, *Epit. Hist.*, XIII, 12, 30–34; this demolition has at times been attributed to the reign of Constantius II, Constantine's successor.

31. Libanius, *Orat.* 30, *Pro temp.*, 6, 39 end.

32. On the prestige of the god of Aigeai and on the destruction of the temple see Louis Robert, "De la Cilicie à Messine et à Plymouth avec deux inscriptions errantes," *Jour. sav.*, 1973, 161–211, esp. 188–193: "we cannot know what local considerations led the emperor or the local authorities to this act of violence against a highly venerated sanctuary." Inscription from Epidaurus: "To Aesclepius Aigeates, the hierophant and priest of the Savior Mnaseas son of Mnaseas, of Hermione, in keeping with a dream" (*IG*, IV2, 1, 438). Libanius: *Autobiography*, 143, with the commentary of P. Petit.

33. Cod. Theod., XV, 12. 1.

4. The Wavering Fourth Century

1. For Bemarchius, see Libanius, I (*Autobiography*), 39. On Libanius and the panegyric to Constantius, see *Orat.* 59, and *Autobiography*, 80.

2. A. Cameron, *Jour. Rom. St.*, 1964, pp. 24 ff., and "Gratian's Repudiation of the Pontifical Robe," ibid., 1966, pp. 96–99, (esp. 99). The episode is omitted by Ammianus Marcellinus, XVI, 10, who describes in detail the emperor's visit (particularly, paras. 15–17, his reactions to the forum of Trajan).

3. Libanius, I (*Autobiography*), 177.

4. Ibid., 173; Ammianus, XVI, 8, 2. The weasel was then a familiar animal, like the cat today.

5. Ammianus, XV, 7, 7–10 (in 355), XXI, 15, 2 (in 361).

6. Ibid., XIX, 12, 12.

7. Held office 357–359; Ammianus, XVI, 10, 17, XVII, 4, 1, for the obelisk; *CIL*, VI, 45 = Dessau, 3222, for the temple of Apollo.

8. Ammianus, XIX, 10, 4.

9. Socrates, III, 2; V, 16. Socrates' *Hist. Eccles.* ends in 439. He obviously began writing long before that date and made at least one revision of this book. Sozomen, another church historian, who was a contemporary of Socrates and clearly made use of him, talks of nothing but "ridiculous and bizarre statues and instruments" (V, 7, 6).

10. R. Turcan, *Mithra et le mithriacisme* (Paris, 1981), p. 92.

11. Julian, *Letter* 79 Bidez.

12. Socrates, *Hist. Eccl.*, III, 2; Theodoret, *Hist. Eccl.*, III, 18, 1; and Sozomen, *Hist. Eccl.*, V, 7; as well as Ammianus, XII, 11, 3–11, and Julian, *Letter* 60.

13. Ammianus, XXI, 14, 2–5. On the fears of Christians at a later period regarding former local deities, see Chapter 8, the section on "Return to Alexandria."

14. See Theodoret, *Hist. Eccl.*, III, 7, 5 ff. (8 for the story of Marcus), and Libanius, *Letter* 819, 6, of 363. Compare the martyrdom of the Christian schoolteacher Cassianus, who was killed by his pupils with their styluses, as told by Prudentius, *Book of Crowns (Peristephanon)*, IX, v. 13–15.

15. Sozomen, *Hist. Eccl.*, V, 15, 4–10.

16. Julian, *Letter* 114. See G. W. Bowersock, *Roman Arabia* (Cam-

bridge, Mass., 1983), pp. 125–127; M. Sartre, *Bostra des origines à l'Islam* (Paris, 1985), pp. 104 ff.

17. Eunapius, *Lives of the Sophists*, VI, 2.

18. J. and J. C. Balty, "Julien et Apamée. Aspects de la restauration de l'hellénisme et de la politique antichrétienne de l'empereur," *Dialogues d'histoire ancienne* I (1974): 276–304; J. Balty, *Mosaïques antiques de Syrie* (Brussels, 1977), pp. 78–80, 88–89.

19. J. and J. C. Balty think that because of the arrangement of its letters, the Greek expression "use well" is a parody of Christ's monogram surrounded by the alpha and the omega.

20. Socrates, III, 18.

21. G. W. Bowersock, *Julian the Apostate* (Cambridge, Mass., 1978), p. 93.

22. Julian, *Misopogon*, 357 c; cf. Theodoret, *Hist. Eccl.*, III, 7, 5; Philostorgius, p. 229 Bidez.

23. Julian, *Letter 84* Bidez (on "houses for guests," *xenodocheia*, see E. Kislinger, "Kaiser Julian und die [christlichen] Xenodocheia," *Festschrift H. Hunger* [Vienna, 1984], pp. 171–184); Greg. Naz., *Orat.* 5 112 (*PG* 35, 649). In the same meaning, cf. the Christian historian Sozomen, V, 16, to whom we owe the text of this letter. The quotation from Saint Ambrose comes from G. Boissier, *Fin du paganisme*, II, 336. For a good commentary on Julian's initiatives, see ibid., I, 167 ff.

24. Eunapius, *Lives of the Sophists*, XXIII, 2, 7–8; 4.

25. Bowersock, *Julian*, pp. 116 ff. For a recent interpretation of Julian (which is no longer the last one), see A. Momigliano, "The Disadvantages of Monotheism for a Universal State," *Class. Phil.*, 1986, pp. 285–297; reprinted in *Ottavo Contributo alla Storia degli Studi Classici e del Mondo Antico*, (Rome, 1987), pp. 313–328.

26. *Leges a me in exordio imperii datae, quibus unicuique, quo animo inbibisset, colendi libera facultas tributa est*, Cod. Theod., IX, 16, 9, from 371.

27. Cod. Theod., X, 1, 8 (February 4?), IX, 16, 7, September 9.

28. Cod. Theod., XVI, 1, 1(365); G. Fowden, "Bishops and Temples in the Eastern Roman Empire, A.D. 320–435," *Journ. Theo. St.*, 1978, pp. 53–78, esp. 57.

29. Ammianus, XXIX, 1, 11.

30. Theodoret, *Hist. Eccl.*, IV, 24, 2 ff. See A. Festugière, *Antioche païenne et chrétienne* (Paris, 1959), p. 271.

31. Cod. Theod., IX, 16, 8; J. Maurice, "Terreur de la magie," pp. 115 ff.; H. Funke, "Majestäts- und Magieprozesse bei Ammianus Marcellinus," *Jahrb. für Ant. und Christ.* (1967), pp. 145–175.

32. On the functions of the vicar of Asia, see L. Robert, *Hellenica* IV (1948): 47.

33. John Chrysostom, *Homily 89 in Acta Apostol.* (*PG*, 60, 274–275).

34. See Ammianus, XXIX, 1, for the entire story; cf. Zosimus, IV, 14.

35. P. Petit, commentary to his edition of Libanius, I (*Autobiography*), 175.

36. Libanius, I (*Autobiography*), 158 ff., 173 ff.

37. Cod. Theod., IX, 16, 9.

38. Ibid., X, 1, 12.

39. Ibid., XVI, 7, 1.

40. For *Dira carmina*, see ibid., XVI, 10, 7.

41. Remark by A. Lippold, "Theodosius I," *Real-Enc.*, *Supp.* XIII (1973), col. 857, ll. 65 ff.

42. *Pretio artis ⟨magis⟩ quam divinitate metienda* (Cod. Theod., XVI, 10, 8).

43. Ernest Will, *Syria* 27 (1950): 261–269.

44. F. Miltner, *Ephesos* (Vienna, 1958), pp. 104–106; *Jahreshefte Oesterr. Arch. Inst.*, 1959, Beibl. 269 ff.; *Année Epigr.*, 1967, 479.

45. On the imperial cult, cf. G. W. Bowersock: "No thinking man ever believed in the divinity of a living emperor . . . and although he could conceive the deification of a deceased emperor, he could never consider an imperial *theos* one of 'the gods'" (G. W. Bowersock, "Greek Intellectuals and the Imperial Cult," *Le culte des souverains dans l'Empire romain* (Geneva, 1972), pp. 179–206, esp. p. 206). What was true in the second century A.D. was all the more so in the fourth.

5. Toward the Interdict

1. A. Cameron, "Gratian's Repudiation of the Pontifical Robe," *Journ. Rom. St.*, 1968, pp. 96–102. The expression "séparation du paganisme et de l'Etat" is from R. Rémondon, *La crise de l'Empire romain* (Paris, 1970), p. 195.

2. Zosimus, IV, 36.

3. Ambrose, *Letter XVII*, 9–10, *cum maiore iam Curia christianorum numero sit referta.* Scholars, particularly J. Geffcken, *Der Ausgang des griechisch-römischen Heidentums* (Heidelberg, 1920), p. 296, n. 39, have challenged this point as partial, by comparing it with Augustine, *Confessions*, VIII, 2, 3, *tota fere Romana nobilitas*, "almost all the Roman nobility" was pagan. But Augustine refers to conditions under Constantius, thirty years earlier. Cf. the discussion in Boissier, *Fin du*

nobility" was pagan. But Augustine refers to conditions under Constantius, thirty years earlier. Cf. the discussion in Boissier, *Fin du paganisme*, II, 315 ff., whose conclusions are inaccurately reported by Geffcken.

4. Symmachus, *Relatio*, III, 10. On the inadequacies of Symmachus' argument and Ambrose's reply, one always reads with pleasure Boissier's pages in *Fin du paganisme*, II, 325–338. The date of Libanius' plea *For the Temples* has been discussed ever since the seventeenth century, Godefroy placing it about 390 and Tillemont in 384.

5. Cod. Theod., XVI, 10, 9; May 25, 385.

6. Ibid., XII, 1, 112.

7. Zosimus, IV, 37, 3. For the date (384 or 386–387?), see G. Fowden, "Bishops and Temples in the Eastern Roman Empire 320–425 A.D.," *Jour. Theo. St.*, 1978, pp. 53–78 (p. 63, n. 5). For "useless agitation," see Libanius, *Orat.*, 49, 3.

8. Libanius, *Letters*, 1351, 3; 1391, 1 (both of 363), a city "dear to the gods." According to P. Petit, *Byzantion*, 1951, pp. 301 ff., followed by Fowden, "Bishops and Temples," p. 66, it was not the prefect Cynegius, but the count (military commander) of the East Deinias who helped Marcellus. In Palmyra, the Allat temple on the outskirts of the town was laid waste and the cult statue, of Greek style, was defaced in a manner quite reminiscent of the old *damnatio memoriae* for imperial portraits. These events seem to have occurred while Cynegius was Praetorian prefect for the East. See B. Gassowska, "Maternus Cynegius, Praefectus Praetorio Orientis and the Destruction of the Allat Temple in Palmyra," *Archeologia* 33 (1982): 107–123.

9. Theodoret, *Hist. Eccl.*, V, 21, 5; cf. Fowden, "Bishops and Temples," pp. 62–64.

10. It is the *synodos ana to ethnos*. After Sozomen, *Hist. Eccl.*, VII, 15, 12–14.

11. Libanius, *For the Temples* (XXX), 8–11.

12. Ibid., 44–46. For Edessa, J. Godefroy in his *editio princeps* of the address in 1656, followed particularly by Petit, *Byzantion*, pp. 298–304.

13. Louis Sébastien Le Nain de Tillemont in his *Histoire des Empereurs* (Paris, 1720), V, 733, and Jacques Schwartz, *Essays B. C. Welles* (New Haven, 1966), I, 104–105.

14. Libanius, XVIII, 214. Carrhae, *oppidum invalidis circumdatum muris*, Amm. Marc., XVIII, 7 , 3; in 359.

15. Luc., *Syr. goddess.* (XLIV), esp. 28, 37–38, 58. On the authen-

ticity and accuracy of the *Syrian goddess*, see C. P. Jones, *Culture and Society in Lucian* (Cambridge, Mass., 1986), pp. 41–45.

16. Julian, *Letter 98;* Egeria, *Travel Journal,* ed. P. Maraval, coll. Sources chrétiennes, no. 296 (Paris, 1982), 18. On the military significance of Hierapolis, see G. Goossens, *Hiérapolis. Essai de monographie historique* (Louvain, 1943), pp. 147–151, the city was "assez proche de la frontière pour former la limite du théâtre d'opérations", "le grand quartier général et le dépôt de mobilisation de l'armée d'Orient" (p. 148).

17. This was pointed out to me by M. Tardieu (by letter). Dimashqi mentions a statue of Mars in iron, as pointed out by Jacques Schwartz, *Essays B. C. Welles;* however, the iron is attributed to Mars simply because he is the god of war, just as the sun, in the same text, has a statue of gold (Dimashqi, in Chwolsohn, *Die Ssabier und der Ssabismus* (St. Petersburg, 1856), II, 388.

18. Cod. Theod., XVI, 3, 1; quoted by F. Thélamon, *Païens et chrétiens au IVe siècle. L'apport de "L'histoire ecclésiastique" de Rufin d'Aquilée* (Paris, 1981), p. 254.

19. Ambrose, *Letter 40,* 6; 13, 16; Paulinus, *Vit. Ambr.,* 22.

20. Pacatus, *Paneg. Lat.,* XII, 1–3, 4, 5, 47.

21. Claudian, *Sixth Consulate of Honorius, Panegyric,* 55 ff.

22. Detailed account in Sozomen, VII, 25; Rufinus, XI, 18; it is Theodoret, V, 17, who gives the numbers of victims.

23. Cod. Theod., II, 8, 19, Aug. 7, 389. Religious policy of the emperor: Lippold, "Theodosius I," cols. 956–958.

24. Cod. Theod., XVI, 10, 10 and 11.

25. Fowden, "Bishops and Temples," p. 70.

26. Socrates (who was their former pupil), V, 16.

27. Alan Cameron, *Claudian. Poetry and Propaganda at the Court of Honorius* (Oxford, 1970), pp. 28 ff.

28. Palladas, in *Anth. Pal.,* IX, 501. These two lines are of doubtful sense, but they seem to express the discouragement of a pagan intellectual seeing his native city bereft of its former gods. I am following the simpler explanation of P. Laurens (in the Budé series, vol. X), opposing A. Cameron, "Palladas and Christian Polemic, *Jour. Rom. St.,* 1975, pp. 17–30 (p. 24), for whom it means: "Dead men [that is, pagan gods in Christian terminology] have left our city, which once was alive. And we, left alive, we officiate at our city's funeral." None of these explanations sounds wholly satisfactorily. Against P. Laurens, the Greek aorist "have left" ought not to be translated as an imperfect, "were [repeatedly] leaving," and the word "once" ought

to bear on "alive." Against A. Cameron, it is harsh to believe that an actual pagan could apply to the gods so injurious a term as "dead men," even in a burst of bitter irony—which perhaps could be oversubtly concealed here.

29. Socrates, V, 17; Sozomen, VII, 15, 9.

30. Ammianus, XXII, 16, 12; Socrates, V, 16; Sozomen, VII, 15.

31. Asclepius, 24. Cf. Augustine, *City of God*, VIII, 23, 26. On the Egyptian background of such utterances, see G. Fowden, *The Egyptian Hermes. A Historical Approach to the Late Pagan Mind* (Cambridge, 1986), pp. 38–44.

32. So A. D. Nock and S. C. Neil, *Jour. Theo. St.*, 1925, pp. 173–176, and again A. D. Nock, introduction to the Asclepius (Budé edition of Hermes Trismegistus, II, 288–289); in the footnotes of the same volume, A. J. Festugière makes the correct statement (p. 379, n. 201).

33. On these destructions, see Rufinus, II, 27, and Eunapius, VI, 11.

34. Paulinus, *Vit. Ambr.*, 26, 36; Rufinus, II, 33; Sozomen, VII, 22; Theodoret, V, 29, 4 (Hercules and the cross); Augustine, *City of God*, V, 26, 1 (statues of Jupiter); see Thélamon, *Païens et chrétiens*, pp. 316–322.

35. Cod. Theod., XVI, 10, 12. The law was renewed at the accession of Arcadius, ibid., XVI, 10, 13, Aug., 7, 395.

36. Ibid., XVI, 10, 14.

37. Zosimus, IV, 59; *CIL.*, VI, 1783 = Dessau 2948.

38. Actian games commemorated the anniversary of the naval victory won near Actium by Octavian (later Augustus) over Antony and Cleopatra, September 2, 31 B.C.

6. After the Defeat

1. Augustine, *City of God*, 18, 54; *Enarr. in Psalmis*, 98, 14.

2. Cod. Theod., XVI, 10, 17, and 18.

3. Augustine, Sermon XXIV, 6 (shaving off Hercules' beard); *Letter* 50 (Sufes' riots); *Letter* 91, 8 (Calama).

4. Quodvultdeus, ed. R. Braun (Paris, 1964, coll. Sources chrétiennes, nos. 101–102), text vol. II, *Liber promiss. Dei*, III, para. 44; cf. introduction, I, 70–72. It seems to me that Quodvultdeus himself offers the explanation of the destruction of the temple transformed

into a church: *Cumque a quodam pagano falsum vaticinium velut eiusdem Caelestis proferretur, quo rursus et via et templa prisco sacrorum ritui redderetur.* He was writing from his refuge in Campania around 450 after Carthage had been taken by the Vandals (439). On the total disappearance of the temple and its avenue in the general devastation of Carthage, see also Victor, bishop of Vita in Byzacene (region of Sousse in modern Tunisia): the Vandals "have completely razed the odeon, the theater, the temple of Memory, and the avenue known as Caelestis" (*Hist. persec. Afric. prov.*, ed. M. Petschenig, [Vienna, 1881], I, 8. For the situation in general, P. Courcelle, *Histoire littéraire des grandes invasions germaniques*, 3rd ed. (Paris, 1964), pp. 136–139.

5. Cod. Theod., XV, 6, 1, and 2.

6. Ibid., XVI, 10, 15.

7. Ibid., XV, 1, 36.

8. John Chrysostom, *Letters* 123 and 126 (*PG*, vol. 52, 676–678, 685–687); see also Theodoret, *Hist. Eccl.*, V, 29. It is much more doubtful that Chrysostom acted also against pagans at Ephesus; see C. Baur, *Joh. Chrysost. und seine Zeit*, II, 132 ff., 328–333.

9. Cod. Theod., XVI, 10, 16.

10. John Chrysostom, *Homil. in Matth.*, LXX [LXXI], 5 [*PG*, vol. 58, 660].

11. Marcus the Deacon, *Life of Porphyrius*, trans. and commentary by H. Grégoire and M.-A. Kugener (Paris, 1930). P. Peeters, "La Vie géorgienne de saint Porphyre de Gaza," *Analecta Bollandiana*, 1941, pp. 94–99, has published a Georgian Life of Porphyry and shown conclusively that it was translated from an older one, in Syriac, that differs in some respects from the Greek text (about which it is difficult to believe that it has a Syriac origin). See also note 42.

12. Fowden, "Bishops and Temples," pp. 72–75. For still active temples, see Marcus the Deacon, *Porphyrius*, 26.

13. Marcus the Deacon, *Porphyrius*, paras. 19, 17.

14. Ibid., para. 41.

15. Ibid., paras. 47–50, 63–70.

16. Ibid., para. 76.

17. Ibid., paras. 95–99; see the introduction by Grégoire and Kugener, pp. lxviii-lxx.

18. Cod. Theod., XVI, 10, 22.

19. Temple of Aphrodite, see A. Dagron, *Naissance d'une capitale*, p. 375. For the law, see Cod. Theod., XVI, 10, 19, from 408, addressed to the pretorian prefect in Rome. G. Fowden has a different interpretation in "Bishops and Temples," p. 65, n. 2: "temples on the

imperial estates were already beginning to be demolished systematically." The use of disaffected temples as military barracks is much older than the proscription of paganism.

20. L. Robert, *Hellenica,* IV (1948), p. 95 (and pp. 41, 60, 73). See also H. Blumenthal, "529 and Its Sequel," *Byzantion* (1978): 369–385 (373–375 on Plutarchus, identifying the sophist of the inscription with the philosopher).

21. Callinicus, *Life of Hypatius,* ed. G. J. M. Bartelink (Paris, 1971, Sources chrétiennes, no. 177), chap. 33.

22. Cod. Theod., XVI, 10, 25.

23. Callinicus, *Life of Hypatius,* chaps. 30, 1–2. For the Rhebas, see ibid., chap. 45. A. H. M. Jones, "Social Background of the Struggle," p. 18, is surprised by the contrast between Pliny, *Letters,* X, 96, 9–10, and the *Life of Hypatius.* Shortly after Pliny Lucian also, in *Alexander, or the False Prophet,* mentions the Christians of Pontus and Bithynia.

24. Augustine, *Letters,* 97, 2.

25. Zosimus, V, 38, with commentary by F. Paschoud.

26. On the Sibylline Books, see Rutilius Namatianus, *On his Return,* II, 52. See Cameron, *Claudian,* pp. 220 ff., which cites Saint Melanie. On the statue of the Victory, see ibid., pp. 237–240.

27. Eunapius, fr. 62 Müller, preserved by Constantine Porphyrogenitus and followed by Zosimus, V, 1, 1–3; 12. On Eunapius' violent hostility toward Stilico, see Photius, cod. 98; Olympiodorus, followed by Zosimus in V, 34 (see the notes by F. Paschoud). On Claudian, who probably died in 404, see Cameron, *Claudian,* passim.

28. Zosimus, V, 41; cf. Sozomen, IX, 6, 4. The resort to Etruscan haruspices, and their use of lightning as a weapon, was quite traditional in republican Rome. On Gabinius' end, see *Life of Saint Melanie,* ed. D. Gorce, (Paris, 1962, Sources chrétiennes, no. 40), para. 19.

29. Zosimus, VI, 7, 4.

30. On the *Oraculum,* see J. Flamant, *Macrobe et le néoplatonisme latin à la fin du VIe siècle* (Leiden, 1977), pp. 109 ff., esp. 116.

31. *Sodales ballatores Cybelae, cantabrarii, signiferi, nemesiaci, virtutiarii:* Cod. Theod., XIV, 7, 2 [3 Haenel] and XV, 7, 13 (in 412 and 413–414). See J. P. Waltzing, *Etude historique sur les corporations professionnelles chez les Romains, depuis les origines jusqu'à la chute de l'Empire d'Occident* (Louvain, 1895), I, 240–253 (the *dendrophori*); II, 138 (the corporations of the spectacle).

32. The house arrest of priests and the confiscation of the holdings of colleges, *frediani, dendrophori,* and other *professiones gentiliciae:* Cod. Theod., XVI, 10, 20.

33. A lively and highly accessible account can be found in Courcelle, *Histoire littéraire*, cited in note 4. Its first edition appeared in 1948, and the author was visibly influenced by the memory of the struggle against Nazi Germany, to which he compares the Vandals. He is more indulgent toward the Franks.

34. "From whatever kind of school," according to Damascius, *Life of Isidore*, cited by the *Souda*. A philosopher himself, Damascius accurately characterized the teaching of Hypatia. See also J. Bregman, *Synesius of Cyrene, Philosopher-Bishop* (Berkeley and London, 1982), pp. 22–25, 36–39. In addition, the expression from the *Souda*, *dia mesou tou asteos*, does not mean that Hypatia made public appearances "in the street," but "in the city" (and not in a less crowded suburb or rural area, as Antoninus had done somewhat earlier). On Antoninus, see Eunapius, *Lives of the Sophists*, VI, 9, 15–17; and 10, 6–10.

35. Cf. John Chrysostom in Festugière, *Antioche païenne et chrétienne*, p. 337, and n. 1.

36. Socrates, VII, 15.

37. J. M. Rist, "Hypatia," *Phoenix* 19 (1965): 214–225.

38. For rioting in the theater, see the sketch in Alan Cameron, *Circus Factions, Blues and Greens at Rome and Byzantium* (Oxford, 1976), pp. 213–229. On violence and theatrical pleasures in Alexandria, see Bowman, *Egypt after the Pharaohs*, pp. 214–216.

39. On the Caesareum, its fate and its meaning for Christians in Alexandria, see Bowman, *Egypt after the Pharaohs*, p. 207.

40. Synesius' letters (10 and 16 are the most fervent) were sent to Hypatia in 404–407, and he followed her classes before 395, at which time he returned to Cyrene. See C. Lacombrade, ed., *Hymns of Synesius*, p. xv.

41. Hugo Pratt, *The Lagoon of Beautiful Dreams*, trans. Rinaldo Traini (New York: Graphic, 1972).

42. Peeters, "Vie géorgienne," pp. 87–88, has shown how, through that story and elsewhere in the lives, Porphyry's hagiographical picture was emulating Cyril's. As Michel Tardieu has pointed out to me, the more concrete character is not the pagan priestess in the Georgian text, but the Manichaean Elected, with her pale complexion (Manichaean Elected were strict vegetarians and fasted often), her "pictorial" gift of persuasion, and her retinue, quite necessary to keep the Elected free of such impure necessities as cooking food and so on (Marcus, *Life of Porphyrius*, pp. 85–90).

43. Principal sources: Socrates, *Hist. Eccles.*, VII, 13–15; Damascius, *Life of Isidorus*, fr. 102 to 105 saved by the excerpts of Photius and the *Souda*-lexicon. For modern literature, see chiefly K.

Praechter, "Hypatia," *Real-Enc.*, 1914, cols. 242–249; Rist, *Phoenix*; Bregman, *Synesius of Cyrene*; I. Hadot, *Arts libéraux et philosophie dans la pensée antique* (Paris, 1984), pp. 259–260.

7. Political Exclusion

1. Cod. Theod., XVI, 5, 42. Remark by J. Geffcken, p. 179.

2. Generid: Zosimus, V, 46, 2–5. Fravitta: Zosimus, V, 20, 1 and 21, 5.

3. Cod. Theod., XVI, 10, 21.

4. Ibid., 22, 23, 24.

5. Alan Cameron, "The Empress and the Poet," *Yale Class. St.*, 1982, p. 217–289, esp. 266.

6. Cod. Theod., XVI, 10, 25; ibid., *Novellae*, III, 8; Cod. Just., I, 11, 7. We should also cite a law, dating perhaps fom 472 (ibid., 8), that reinvokes more harshly the law of 392 prohibiting the cults (Cod. Theod., XVI, 10, 12).

7. Salvian, *De gub. Dei*, VI, 2, 12.

8. A. Lippold, "Theodosius II," *Real-Enc.*, *Supp.* XIII (1972), cols. 961–1044, esp. 1017.

9. Cameron, "Empress and Poet."

10. Ibid., pp. 221–225, 254–270. The Christmas sermon of 441 is quoted and commented on pp. 243 ff.

11. The plural "embassies" is used only by his admirer, the Neoplatonist Hierocles. See Photius, no. 214.

12. Photius, no. 80, 58b-59a (Olympiodorus, fr. 22 Maisano).

13. Ibid., 61a, 62a (Olympiodorus, fr. 41–43, 49–50 Maisano).

14. Damascius, *Life of Isidorus*, fr. 278–283, 303–305 Zintzen. For conspiracies against the emperor in the fifth century, see R. von Haehling, "Damascius und die heidnische Opposition im 5. Jahrhundert nach Christus," *Jahrb. für Ant. und Christ.* (1980), pp. 82–95.

15. For the agitation of the Isaurians in the fourth century, see Ammianus, XIV, 2 (in 354); XIX, 13, 1 (in 359); XXVII, 9, 6 (in 365–370). Incursions into Galilee: Saint Jerome, *Letter* 114, 1; into Armenia: John Chrysostom, *Letter* 135. More complete references in J. Rougé, "L'Histoire Auguste et l'Isaurie au IVe siècle," *Rev. Et. Anc.*, 1966, pp. 282–315; see also L. Robert, *Documents de l'Asie mineure méridionale* (Geneva and Paris, 1966), pp. 50 ff., 91–100.

16. Photius, no. 242, 290 = Damascius, fr. 303 Zintzen. For enumeration of the attempts at restoring paganism, from Julian to Illous, of which the specifics cause problems, see R. Asmus, *Byz. Zeitschr*,

1909, p. 468, and the article Fl. Zeno 6 in *PLRE II* (the "commander in chief for the East" of whom Damascius speaks would be Zeno, antagonistic to negotiating with Attila: Priscus, fr. 14 and John of Antioch, fr. 199).

17. For these events, see the corresponding entries in *PLRE II*, in particular "Fl. Zeno 7" and "Fl. Ardabur Aspar."

18. E. W. Brooks, "The Emperor Zeno and the Isaurians," *English Hist. Rev.*, 1893, pp. 209–238; H. Grégoire, "Au camp d'un Wallenstein byzantin, La vie et les vers de Pamprépios, aventurier païen," *Bull. Assoc. G. Budé* 24 (1929): 22–38; R. Keydell, "Pamprepius," *Real-Enc.* (1949), cols. 409–415; E. Livrea, edition of Pamprepius' poetry, Leipzig (coll. Teubner), 1979; R. M. Harrison, "The Emperor Zeno's Real Name," *Byz. Zeitschr*, 1981, pp. 27–28.

19. Zacharias Scholasticus, *Life of Severus*, ed. and trans. M.-A. Kugener (Paris, 1905, Patrologia Orientalis, II, 1), p. 40.

8. Masters and Pupils, or the Appeal of Paganism

1. Zacharias Scholasticus, *Life of Severus*, p. 67. The original, written between 512 and 518, was in Greek.

2. Marinus of Neapolis, *Life of Proclus*, trans. K. S. Guthrie (New York, 1925; rpt. Chicago, 1977).

3. Ibid., 11 (arrival in Athens), 15 (sojourn in Lydia). The enemies of Proclus were identified as Christians by H. Saffrey, "Allusions antichrétiennes chez Proclus le diadoque néoplatonicien," *Revue des Sciences Philosophiques et Théologiques* 59 (1975): 553–563; see also M. Tardieu, *Les Paysages reliques. Routes et haltes syriennes d'Isidore à Simplicius* (Paris and Louvain, 1990), Introduction, n. 13.

4. Marinus of Neapolis, *Life of Proclus*, 18-end, 19, 28–30.

5. Zacharias, *Life of Severus*.

6. On the mobility of students, see Alan Cameron, "The End of the Ancient Universities," *Cahiers d'histoire mondiale*, 1967, pp. 653–673, 660; traditionally riotous, ibid., p. 654.

7. Zacharias, *Life of Severus*, pp. 14–20. The charms of Canopus are described in a beautiful passage in Strabo, XVII, 1, 16–17 (800 ff). On the region, see A. Bernand, *Alexandrie la Grande* (Paris, 1966), pp. 132 ff., and *Le Delta égyptien d'après les textes grecs, 1. Les Confins libyques* (Cairo, 1970), pp. 153–328, esp. 243, 291 ff., 322 ff.

8. Zacharias, *Life of Severus*, pp. 20–22.

9. Ibid., pp. 23–26.

10. Ibid., pp. 27–32.

11. Ibid., pp. 32–35. The word "surgeons" (or "bone-setters," Copt. *karoumtitin*, that is, Greek *keromatites*), has been explained by Eduard Schwartz, *Sitz. Heidelb. Akad.*, 1912, 16, p. 27. See more instances in L. Robert, *Hellenica* XIII (1965): 167–170. Those would-be healing gods are unable to heal themselves—a glimpse into the last role held by those deities, dispensation of health; cf. Proclus' relationship to Asclepius.

12. See the commentary by J. Maspero, "Horapollon et la fin du paganisme égyptien," *Bull. inst. fr. arch. or.* 11 (1913): 178, and compare the opening words of the Catholic (Nicaean) Creed: *Credo in unum Deum omnipotentem, creatorem coeli et terrae.*

13. G. Fowden, "The Pagan Holy Man in Late Antique Society," *Journ. Hell. St.*, 1982, pp. 33–59, esp. 54, attributes Horapollo's apostasy to his problems with the police. Damascius says precisely the opposite.

14. *Souda*, under Harpocras and Horapollo; Damascius, cod. 242; Photius, 292 (fr. 313–316 Zintzen). On these episodes, see Tardieu, *Paysages reliques*, chap. 1, nn. 4, 9.

15. *PLRE*, II, Hormisdas.

16. Zacharias, *Life of Severus*, p. 77.

17. Nonnus, *Dionysiaca*, 41, 143–151.

18. Zacharias, *Life of Severus*, pp. 58–65.

19. Homosexuality was more readily tolerated by the pagans than by the Christians. The *Souda* glosses *pornos* as "idolater," which is one meaning of the word as used by Zacharias. Nonnus is the last author to speak openly about it. At the time of Justinian, the licentious poems of Paul the Silentiary pretend to be unaware of homosexual relations, whereas his poetry (if not his actual behavior) respects no other taboos (including anal intercourse with women).

20. I. Hadot, *Philosophie et Arts libéraux* (Paris, 1984), chap. VI, "L'enkuklios paideia": la notion et son contenu," pp. 263–293.

21. Zacharias, *Life of Severus*, p. 67. See earlier in this chapter (at note 1) Leontius' horoscope predicting the birth of a boy and the precaution taken by him.

22. Zacharias, *Life of Severus*, pp. 66, 68 ff., 73; Damascius, *Life of Isidorus*, cod. 242 Photius, 46; see *PLRE* II, Leontius 14, which does not see the similarity with the *magistros* Leontius known to Zacharias.

23. Chrysaorius and the sacristan were taken by surprise at the time of the feast of Saint John the Baptist. This tremor cannot be dated. Because Severus and Zacharias studied in Beirut between 487

and 491, it cannot have been the shock of 494 (P. L. Gatier, "Tremblements du sol et frissons des hommes. Trois séismes en Orient sous Anastase," *Tremblements de terre. Histoire et archéologie* (Valbonne, 1984), pp. 87–94, esp. 91, n. 5.

24. N. G. Wilson, *Scholars of Byzantium* (London, 1983), pp. 30–33. On Gaza, there is a monograph by G. Downey, *Gaza in the Early Sixth Century* (Norman, Okla., 1963).

25. H. Diels, *Ueber die von Prokop beschriebene Kunstuhr von Gaza*, Abhand. der Königlich. Preuss. Akad. der Wiss., 1917, no. 7 (with the text and a German translation of the work). It is hard to follow H. Stierlin, *L'astrologie et le pouvoir* (Paris, 1986), pp. 235–243, on the daring it must have taken to write a description of such a clock and on the censorship that must have stripped Procopius' text of its astronomical-astrological data. The public of the time was very excited about mechanical instruments, automatons such as those described by Nonnus (*Dion.*, 3, 169–179), or an organ like the one Boethius constructed at Theodoric's request.

26. P. Friedländer, *Spätantiker Gemäldezyklus in Gaza* (Vatican, 1939), pp. 24 ff. for the Rosalia.

27. Photius, cod. 160, 102b.

28. Choricius, ed. R. Förster (Leipzig, 1929).

29. Compare Pierre Chuvin, "Les fondations syriennes de Séleucos Nicator dans la *Chronique* de Jean Malalas," *Actes de la table ronde "Géographie historique du Proche-Orient"* (Paris and Valbonne, 1987), pp. 99–110.

30. F. Paschoud, Foreword to vol. I of his edition of Zosimus, (Paris, 1971), p. xiv–xvii and xx.

31. Ibid., pp. xxiv ff.

32. See Tardieu, *Paysages reliques*, chap. 1 (Iamblichus and Damascius at the sacred waters in southern Syria) and chap. 3 (Simplicius and Khabur's springs).

9. The Fragmented West

1. Damascius, *Life of Isidorus*, cod. 242 Photius, 91; same remark regarding the assassination of Aetius, the conqueror of Attila in 451, a friend of Marcellinus.

2. *Souda*, I, 282, 9 ff., III, 325, 30 ff. = Damascius, fr. 144 and 159 Zintzen. Compare Epictetus, *Discourses*, III, 6, 10.

3. Damascius, *Life of Isidorus*, 108, 64.

4. Claudian, *Consulship of Stilico*, III, pref., 19; 202–216; *VI Consulship of Honorius*, 597–599.

5. In 483, the restoration of a statue of Minerva in Rome, CIL, VI, 1, 526 = 1664 = Dessau 3132; Geffcken, 181.

6. Invincible, not just "unvanquished." Cited by Peter Brown, "Aspects of the Christianization of the Roman Aristocracy," *Jour. Rom. St.* (1961): 1–11, esp. 4; cf. E. Stein, *Histoire du Bas-Empire* II. *De la disparition de l'Empire d'Occident à la mort de Justinien, 476–665* (Paris and Brussels, 1949), p. 44.

7. Courcelle, *Histoire littéraire des grandes invasions germaniques*, p. 249.

8. Firmicus Maternus, *L'erreur des religions païennes*, ed. R. Turcan (Paris, 1982).

9. Augustine, *Confessions*, VII, 9, 13; VIII, 2, 3–5. P. Hadot, *Marius Victorinus, recherches sur sa vie et ses oeuvres* (Paris, 1971; Etudes Augustiniennes), p. 14 (pp. 215–231 on the problem of his influence over pagans).

10. A. Cameron, "Paganism and Literature in Fourth Century Rome," *Christianisme et formes littéraires de l'Antiquité tardive*, Fondation Hardt, Entretiens, vol. XXIII (Geneva, 1976), pp. 1–40, esp. 20–22.

11. *Epigrammata Bobiensia*, ed. W. Speyer (Leipig, 1963), II, 5. Quotation cited by Brown, "Aspects of the Christianization," p. 1.

12. *Carmen contra paganos*, ed. G. Manganaro, *Nuovo Didaskaleion* II (1961): 23–45; see J. F. Matthews, "The Historical Setting of the *carmen contra paganos*," *Historia* (1970): 464–479, and L. Cracco Ruggini, *Il paganesimo romano tra religione e politica (384–394 d.C.): per una reinterpretazione del* Carmen contra paganos (Rome, 1979; Acc. Naz. dei Lincei, Memorie, VIII, 23, 1), in whose view the poem, written in 384, was directed against Vettius Agorius Praetextatus.

13. Zosimus, V, 41, 1–3. J. F. Matthews, *Western Aristocracies and Imperial Court, A.D. 364–424* (Oxford, 1975), pp. 242, 290.

14. Salvian, *Government of God*, VI, 1, 12.

15. CIL, VI, 1783 = Dessau 2948. On this movement of conversion, see Brown, "Aspects of the Christianization."

16. Brown, "Aspects of the Christianization," p. 11.

17. Leo, *Sermon 27, 14, On the birth of the Lord*, 7; PL, 54, 218 ff.; see P. Courcelle, *Les Lettres grecques en Occident de Macrobe à Cassiodore* (Paris, 1943), p. 35 (reference made by Flamant, *Macrobe et le néoplatonisme latin*, p. 676), and primarily Dölger, *Sol Salutis*, chap. 1, and pp. 258, 404.

18. *Letter* 100, ed. G. Pomarès, Sources Chrétiennes, no. 65 (1959), particularly paras. 10–19, 23 (misery of Africa, Gaul, and Italy, while the East "abounds in wealth of every kind," *omnium rerum copiis exuberat et abundat*).

19. Gregory, *Correspondence*, XI, 34; quoted by C. Dagens, *Saint Grégoire le Grand. Culture et expérience chrétiennes* (Paris, 1977; Etudes augustiniennes), pp. 31–32. "Grammar" included what we call literature. We should add that this observation is not enough to encompass Gregory's attitude toward literary culture, as pointed out by P. Riché as well. See P. Riché, *Ecoles et enseignement dans le Haut Moyen Age* (Paris, 1979), pp. 17–18, 26–35.

20. For an example of this difficulty, see what is said in the *Historia Augusta* concerning solar and other devotions of Elagabalus and Alexander Severus.

21. After 431, see A. Cameron, *Jour. Rom. St.*, 1966; ca. 425–428, see Flamant, *Macrobe et le néoplatonisme latin*, p. 134.

22. Macrobius, *Sat.*, I, 17–23; A. Cameron, "Paganism and Literature," pp. 26, 189–190; Flamant, *Macrobe et le néoplatonisme latin*, p. 135.

23. Boissier, *Fin du paganisme*, II, 243 ff.

24. Alan Cameron, after his paper in the Hardt *Entretiens*, recognized during the discussion that he had "oversimplified" his position regarding Virgil.

25. Regarding Macrobius, see the examples quoted by Cameron, *Journ. Rom. St.*, 1966, p. 35; cf. Flamant, *Macrobe et le néoplatonisme latin*, pp. 657 ff.

26. Respectively Apollinaris 6 in *PLRE* II and Fl. 14 in *PLRE* I; on the latter, see Cameron, "Paganism and Literature," p. 13. See also A. Momigliano, in *Problèmes d'historiographie ancienne et moderne* (Paris, 1983), pp. 143 ff. [1969 text] on the subject of late translators of Philostratus, and C. P. Jones, *Journ. Hell. Stud.*, 1980, pp. 190–194.

27. Courcelle, *Lettres grecques*, pp. 235–246.

28. On Vivarium, see Courcelle, ibid., pp. 313–388; more generally, see L. D. Reynolds and N. G. Wilson, *Scribes and Scholars: A Guide to the Transmission of Greek and Latin Literature* (Oxford, 1968).

29. J. Geffcken, *Zwei griechische Apologeten* (Leipzig and Berlin, 1904), p. 321; Martin of Braga, *De correctione rusticorum* (written shortly after 572), ed. C. W. Barlow (New Haven, 1950), chap. 7 ff.

30. Vigilius of Thapsa in Africa (end of fifth century), *Dialogue against the Arians*, I, 5 (*PL*, 62, 157d), quoted and commented on by A. Boulouis, "Références pour la conversion du monde païen aux

VIIe et VIIIe siècles: Augustin d'Hippone, Césaire d'Arles, Grégoire le Grand," *Rev. Et. Aug.*, 1987, pp. 90–112.

31. Gregory, *Correspondence*, IV, 23–26, 29, V, 41, XI, 22.

32. F. H. Dudden, *Gregory the Great. His Place in History and Thought* (London, 1905), II, 127.

33. Gregory, *Correspondence*, III, 59, VIII, 18; cf. IX, 34.

34. Compare Pierre Chuvin, "Nos ancêtres les Grecs," *L'Histoire* 96 (January 1987): 26–32.

10. The Tenacity of the East

1. Stein, *Histoire du Bas-Empire*, pp. 369–375.

2. Cod. Just., I, 5, law 12, chap. 4.

3. Cod. Just., I, 10, laws 1, 2.

4. Cod. Just., I, 11, law 10, passim.

5. Text of the edict reproduced by Lactantius and Eusebius. See Boissier, *Fin du paganisme*, I, 55–63.

6. Cod. Just., I, 5, laws 12, 14 (cf. 18, 19); *Novella 37*, quoted by C. Diehl, *Justinien et la civilization byzantine au VIe siècle* (Paris, 1901), pp. 553 ff. (see pp. 327 ff., 547–566, on pagans in general).

7. Stein, *Histoire du Bas-Empire*, 371, after Malalas, XVIII, 71 Jeffreys (473–474 Dindorf), with the Slavonic chronicle (ed. Spinka, 1940, p. 133), which made it possible to rediscover the original text by Malalas; Stein, *Histoire du Bas-Empire*, 371 n. 1. For Malalas, the latest translation is by E. Jeffreys et al. (Melbourne, 1989). On the Nika sedition, see A. Cameron, *Procopius* (London, 1985), pp. 23, 244 ff.

8. Malalas, XVIII, 42 Jeffreys (449 Dindorf); Theophanes, year of the world 6022, p. 180, ed. C. de Boor (Leipzig, 1883–1885); Procopius, *Anecd.*, 11, 31 ff.; John of Ephesus, *Hist Eccles.*, ed. F. Nau, *Rev. de l'Or. Chrét.*, 1897, p. 481.

9. *Sic* Alan Cameron, "The Last Days of the Academy at Athens," *Proc. Cambridge Philological Soc.*, 195 (1969), p. 7–29.

10. On the existence of these donors, see Damascius, *Life of Isidorus*, fr. 265 Zintzen, from the *Souda*.

11. Libanius, *Autobiography*, 16–29; Synesius, *Letter 135* (PG, 66, 1524 c); quoted by Blumenthal, "529 and Its Sequel," 369–385, esp. 372. Synesius contrasts Athens with Egypt (Alexandria) which welcomed Hypatia and prospered.

12. *Life of Isidorus*, fr. 266 Zintzen.

13. Christodorus, quoted by John of Lydia, *Magistrates*, III, 26 Wünsch.

14. Cod. Just., I, 5, 18 (of 529), I, 11, 9, 10 (not dated; later period); cf. Cameron, "End of the Ancient Universities," pp. 653–673, esp. 670.

15. Cameron, "Last Days of the Academy," p. 14; "End of the Ancient Universities," p. 671.

16. Cameron, "Last Days of the Academy," pp. 11 ff., 13 ff.

17. On the link between medicine and philosophy in Late Antiquity, cf. L. G. Westerink, "Philosophy and Medicine in Late Antiquity," *Janus*, 1964, pp. 169–177, quoted by M. Tardieu, "Sabiens coraniques et 'Sabiens' de Harran," *Journal Asiatique*, 1986, pp. 1–44, esp. 22, n. 99.

18. Epigram in Agathias, II, 31, 7, and in *Anth. Pal.*, IX, 498. Cf. Euripides, *Andromache*, 173–175 ("Barbarians" in general); Diogenes Laertius, *Prologue*, VI, 7, on the Zoroastrian laws regarding funerals and incest, the two being closely related as in Agathias (after Sotion, a peripatetic from Alexandria, 2nd century B.C.); Plutarch, *De fortitudine Alexandri*, I, 5 (328 C): Alexander taught the Persians to venerate their mothers and not to marry them. Historic examples: Artaxerxes II and his daughter Atossa, by whom he had another daughter, Amastris (Plutarch, *Artaxerxes*, 27); the Sogdian governor of Nautaca (Er-Kurgan), Sisimithres, had children by his mother (Quintus-Curtius, VIII, 2, 19). A scandal: Augustus sent to Phraates IV an Italian slave, Musa, by whom he had a son; the son, who became Phraates V, married his mother (Fl. Jos., *Jewish Antiquities*, XVIII, 42 ff.; Lucan, *Pharsalia*, VIII, 401–410; Minucius Felix, *Octavia*, 31, 3; *Orac. Sib.*, VII, 38–50). These extreme forms of endogamy, which have Elamite roots, encountered no obstacle in Zorastrian laws—it is the *khvaetvadatha*, treated by M. Boyce, *A History of Zoroastrianism* (Leiden, 1982), II, 75–77, 220; they were later obfuscated by Islamic sources, after Iranians, like Tabari, had converted to Islam, yet wanted to preserve the greatness of their national past. Nevertheless, compare in Jahiz the polemic between an Arab and a Persian (documentation provided by F. Grenet). On the use of the theme of incestuous unions in the polemics between the Romans and the Sassanians, see H. Chadwick, "The Relativity of Moral Codes: Rome and Persia in Late Antiquity," *Early Christian Literature and the Classical Intellectual Tradition. In honorem Robert M. Grant* (Paris, 1979), pp. 135–153.

19. Interpretation of the expression *eph'heautois* in Agathias by I. Hadot, "La vie et l'oeuvre de Simplicius d'après des sources grecques et arabes," *Simplicius, sa vie, son oeuvre, sa survie* (Berlin and New York, 1987), pp. 3–39, esp. 8.

20. *Anth. Pal.*, VII, 553. Cameron, "Last Days of the Academy," p. 21.

21. Egeria, *Travel Journal*, 20.

22. Procopius, II, 13, 7.

23. Tardieu, "Sabiens," pp. 23, 24 ff.; "Les calendriers en usage à Harran d'après les sources arabes et le commentaire de Simplicius à la *Physique* d'Aristote," in Hadot, *Simplicius*, pp. 40–57, esp. 56.

24. Tardieu, "Sabiens," p. 13.

25. Ibid., pp. 25 ff; see also p. 39. If one finds among the Sabians of Harran roughly the same Platonic references as among the Gnostics, it is because they shared the philosophic culture of Late Antiquity. Nonetheless, they were two totally separate groups.

26. Al-Nadim in D. Chwolsohn, *Die Ssabier und der Ssabismus* (Saint Petersburg, 1856), II, 8; Tardieu, "Calendriers," pp. 53–55.

27. Tardieu, "Sabiens," p. 9 and n. 29. For translations of Greek philosophy in Baghdad, see ibid., nn. 99, 107, which would overturn the theories accepted since M. Meyerhoff, *Archeion* (1933), pp. 1–15.

28. Agathias, *Hist.*, II, 28–31; Malalas, XVIII, 47 Jeffreys (451 Dindorf). See Averil Cameron, *Dumbarton Oaks Papers* 23 (1969): 67–183; *Agathias* (Oxford, 1970), pp. 101–105.

29. H. Blumenthal, "529 and Its Sequel," p. 385.

30. Marinus, *Life of Proclus*, 19; Damascius, *Life of Isidorus*, cod. 242 Photius, 198; Dittenberger, *OGIS*, II, no. 610.

31. John of Ephesus cited in note 8, pp. 490 ff.

32. Procopius, *Wars*, I, 19, 34–37; Etienne Bernand, *Les inscriptions grecques et latines de Philae, II. Haut et Bas Empire* (Paris, 1969), nos. 188–200 and commentary, esp. pp. 32, 241–245; 251; Averil Cameron, *Procopius*, p. 121.

33. Procopius, *Buildings*, VI, 2, 14–20; cf. Cameron, *Procopius*, p. 89; D. Roques, *Synésios de Cyrène et la Cyrénaïque du Bas-Empire* (Paris, 1987), pp. 121, 320 ff. (isolation of Augila "without contact with the [coastal] Pentapolis," which was christianized as early as Julian's reign), 338 ff.

34. Agathias, II, 17, V, 16, regarding Tralles. For evangelism, see John of Ephesus, *Hist. Eccl.*, ed. E. W. Brooks (Louvain, 1964), III, 3, 36.

35. Altan Gökalp, *Têtes rouges et bouches noires. Une confrérie tribale de l'ouest anatolien* (Paris, 1980).

36. Stein, *Histoire du Bas-Empire*, II, 799 ff.; cf. extracts published by F. Nau, *Rev.de l'Or Chrét.*, 1897, p. 482. Regarding the situation of the Monophysites, cf. Diehl, *Justinien*, p. 332, "between the pope and Theodora, Justinian was thoroughly embarrassed."

37. John of Ephesus, III, 3, 27–34 Brooks. The shorter account by Evagrius of Pontus, V. 18, is at some variance with John's. Evagrius was unaware of the events in the Bekaa and in Edessa; the riots were heralded by an earthquake that devastated Daphne. He insists on the relationship between the bishop of Antioch and the governor Anatolius, which led Tiberius to submit the case to the courts in the capital. The "miracle of the icon" is not the same: Anatolius, counterfeiting a suppliant, prays to an image of the Virgin attached to a cord; the Mother of God turns away, refusing to look at the infidel. In Constantinople the people revolted because the accused were condemned to exile and not to death. Evagrius confirms that the emperor and the patriarch were threatened. The Virgin is supposed to have appeared to a courtier who was defending Anatolius, asking him how long he was going to lend his support to someone who offended her and her son. Like John of Ephesus, Evagrius was a witness to the events. What makes John's account so interesting is that it does not limit itself to high personages and provides all too rare glimpses of the situation in the provinces.

38. Constantine Porph., *De administr. imperio*, 50.

Epilogue

1. I am merely following here some of Michel Tardieu's remarkable conclusions in two articles, "Pletho Arabicus, identification et contenu du manuscrit arabe d'Istanbul, Topkapi Serai, Ahmet III 1896," *Jour. As.* (1980); 35–57 (with J. Nicolet), and "Pléthon lecteur des oracles," *Mètis* 2 (1987): 141–164.

2. E. Wind, *Pagan Mysteries in the Renaissance* (London, 1958), a masterly book on the subject.

· INDEX ·